Better Homes and Garde

Landscaping your Garden

Roger Mann

MURDOCH BOOKS®
Sydney • London • Vancouver

Contents

Designing a garden 6
Planning the garden 6
Birds in the garden 13
Working with a designer 14

Putting it on paper 16
Getting it on the ground 24

Design for the climate 28
A temperate climate garden 30
A dry climate 31
A subtropical garden 33
Saving water 34

Front gardens 36
Terrace house front gardens 39
Streetsides and nature strips 40
Australian gardens 42

Types of gardens 44
Formal gardens 44
Informal, flowery gardens 46
Gardens on hillsides 47
Bushland gardens 49
City gardens 51
Low maintenance gardens 54
Native gardens 59
Seaside gardens 62
Kitchen gardens 64
Making a period garden 66

Plants and planting 68
Large shrubs 70
Hedges 71
Climbers 72
Annuals and small shrubs 73
Groundcovers 75
Trees 76
Remodelling an existing garden 78

Colour in the garden 80
Red 81
Blue 82
Pink 83
Yellow 84
Orange 85
White 86
Children's gardens 87

Garden construction 88
Pools and ponds 88
Patios and terraces 90
Barbecues 92
Swimming pools 93
Spas and hot tubs 94
Floors and paving 95
Steps and walls 97
Pergolas 99
Fences and enclosures 101
Ornaments and furniture 103
Lighting the garden 105
Watering systems 105
Costs and budget 106
Legal matters 107

Index 108

...strength may wield the ponderous spade,
May turn the clod, and wheel the compost home;
But Elegance, chief grace the garden shows,
And most attractive, is the fair result
Of Thought, the creature of a polished mind.
William Cowper, 1731–1800

Creating Your Ideal Garden

Once upon a time, 'landscaping' meant just covering as much as possible of the yard with fast-growing grass and then prettying it up with a shrub or two and maybe a flower bed along the front path — or covering everything with gravel or pine chips and adorning that with some bush rocks and native shrubs — hoping that it would all add enough to the value of the property to sweeten the boring task of gardening.

But nowadays most of us expect more from our garden than that it just look pretty. We want to use it as living space — we want a comfortable place where the children can play; where we can entertain our friends; where we can grow some cabbages or daisies if that is our fancy; or maybe just sit and enjoy the environment we have created for ourselves, where the sun and shade are arranged just as we want them.

It isn't at all difficult to create a garden that fits your lifestyle. You can make it formal or casual or cottage; park-like with trees and grass or enclosed and private; a place where you can indulge in the delights of growing things or one which takes just the minimum of care to look its best; you might even decide to recreate your own patch of bushland. You don't need to be a knowledgable gardener, or even a particularly enthusiastic one — imagination and careful planning count for more.

Let this book guide you through the process; it's designed both to stimulate your creativity and to give you practical advice at every stage, so that turning dreams into reality will be as enjoyable as it should be.

Roger Mann

ROGER MANN

INSIDE FRONT COVER: *The ultimate in romance — a border filled with old fashioned roses and irises leading to a lacy gate and who knows what delights beyond.*

FACING PAGE: *Massed irises lending colour and beauty to a gravel path.*

Designing a Garden

Many, perhaps most, of us fall into designing a garden almost by accident. We build or buy a house, and find it sitting on a plot of ground waiting to be transformed into a garden.

The garden designer's palette is the richest offered to any artist — he has the resources of the natural world at his disposal
Thomas Church

"If you're in a slight daze Don't enter this maze"

A CANVAS UMBRELLA *shelters the lunch table in a paved but luxuriantly planted garden — a green oasis in the city.*

How to go about it? The average gardening book tends to discuss the matter only briefly before getting down to vital matters like the best time to plant cabbages. This leaves the first-time garden-maker with the impression that mastery of the ancient (and, it would seem, fiendishly complex) art of gardening is needed before one can even begin.

Happily, that is far from the truth. It isn't difficult to design an attractive garden that will fit your needs and lifestyle, even if you know next to nothing about gardening. This book will show you how.

It isn't a book about gardening — no how to grow cabbages here. It is written from the belief that gardens are intended not just for plants but for people — that what is most important to consider is how you and your family will want to use and enjoy your garden.

Of course, there are pictures of gardens from all over the country to suggest ideas. Some you'll find congenial, others maybe less so — and why not? You are making your garden for your own delight, and if you can't follow your own likes and dislikes here, where can you?

But it is more than just a collection of examples of how other people have made gardens before you. It shows you how to take stock of your own site and needs; how to design in harmony with the sun and wind; how to assess whether a plant will suit your needs; even how to keep track of how much it is all going to cost. If you're nervous about 'design' and making plans, we show you how simple it is to build up a plan from the ideas that come out of just doodling.

And, on the way, there's a little of the philosophy of gardens and garden-making. For the Chinese sage spoke truly when he said that other joys are fleeting — if you would be happy for the rest of your life, make a garden.

Planning the garden

Assessing Your Needs

Sit back and daydream a little. Forget about plants and gardening for a while.... Does the idea of breakfast in the sun on a Sunday morning appeal? Dinner under the stars, in the cool of a summer evening? You might want a sheltered and private patio.

Do you enjoy entertaining? And how far in the future are teenage parties? Will you think of building a permanent barbecue, or would you prefer a portable one? Will you need parking space for your guests? Do you, or the children, like kicking a football around? Rigging up an informal game of tennis? Do you have a dog that likes to romp?

= Designing a garden =

A QUIET PLACE *to sit and enjoy the afternoon, sheltered by trees and greenery.*

THE HAMMOCK *sure looks inviting! This garden is mostly devoted to easy-care trees and groundcovers.*

Games need unencumbered space, and the garden will need to be able to take the punishment.

Consider the family
Are the children still at the tricycle-and-sandpit stage? You might want to create a special space for them, which can be transformed when they grow out of it. Do you need space for hobbies — to build a boat, work on the car, or pull a motorbike to pieces? Do you long for a swimming pool — maybe not now, but when you can afford it? Planning for it now will mean less disruption later.

Do you want to keep chickens? grow vegetables and fruit? Will you be spending much of your free time at home, or would you rather be away sailing, playing golf, or taking holidays? You'll want to plan a garden that can cope with your absence. Or do you just want a quiet place to sit in the shade with a cool drink and a book?

HERBS FOR THE KITCHEN, *grapes for the table (home-made wine, anyone?) and a shady place to sit.*

Landscaping your garden

THINKING OF A GARDEN just in terms of what plants to grow is like designing a house by first choosing the curtains. Just as you consider a house in terms of its rooms — living, dining, bedroom, etc, you can imagine your garden as a sequence of outdoor living rooms. Their 'walls' are made of trees and foliage, the floor is the earth, carpeted with grass or paving, the ceiling is the branches of trees or the open sky, and it's all decorated with flowers and such furniture as you might use.

THE NO-GARDEN GARDEN, *but on a splendid country property like this, its house shaded by century-old trees, is one really needed?*

How much gardening?

How keen are you on gardening — or to put it another way, how important is it to you to have 'a garden that will be the envy of the neighbours' or to achieve the gardening writers' dream of a display of flowers every day of the year? Will the garden be a relaxing hobby or a chore? If you're a reluctant gardener, be warned — enthusiasm may develop as the garden grows and you begin to see the results of your labours; but it's still wise not to plan a garden that will demand more time than you're prepared to give it.

Assessing your site

Before you start transforming your garden into what you would like, take stock of what you have. As the legendary English garden designer Lancelot Brown used to say, back in the eighteenth century: 'Consider the capabilities of the site, M'Lord'. (That's how he got his nickname, Capability Brown.)

Whether you're faced with bare soil and the debris of a just-departed builder, or an established or partially established garden, look around critically — it's surprising how the process will throw up ideas to get you started.

= Designing a garden =

The house sets the theme

Start with the house — do you have big windows looking straight out onto the street or at the neighbours' windows, so that you have to keep your curtains drawn for privacy? Strategically placed foliage might be called for. Not necessarily a dense mass — a clump of airy trees or shrubs will usually be enough to take away the goldfish-bowl feeling and allow you to look out. A group of birches, say, might lead to a woodland theme for the garden; palms to an evocation of a tropical wilderness with a path winding through it to the door.

IT'S RARE *for a house to stand alone without neighbours. In the average street, you're likely to have no less than five properties adjoining your own. Their houses, sheds and trees impinge on your landscape and need to be taken into account in your plans.*

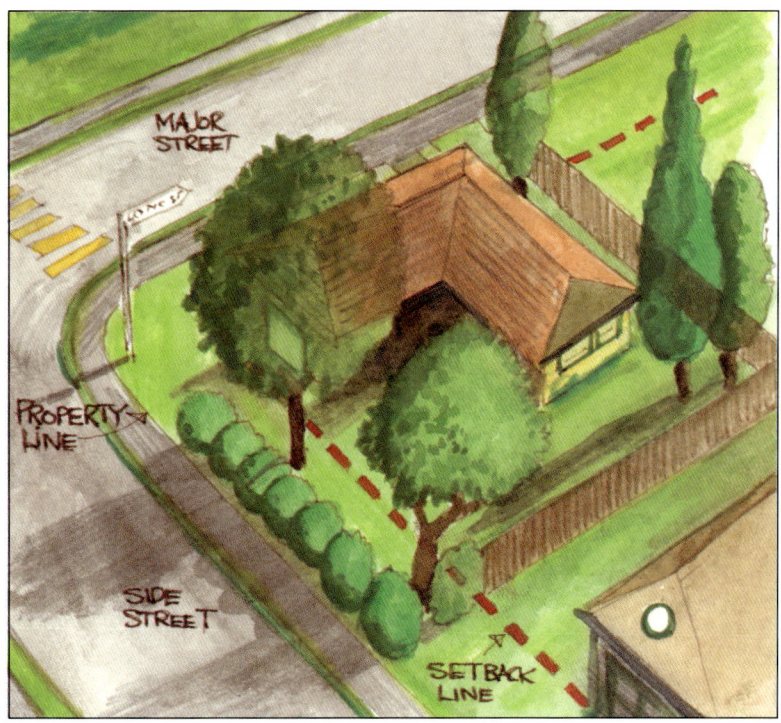

ADORNING THE WALLS *with creepers flatters a handsome old house like this — and can mask the bad features of an ugly one.*

EVEN THE 'FLATTEST' *ground will have some fall. The slope of the ground can be difficult to assess — a 1:1 (45 degrees) slope can look almost vertical from below. If you can see it against the walls of the house, you can measure it against the brick courses.*

ON A CORNER SITE, *you can reclaim a significant amount of private space by planting a row of dense shrubs or a hedge along the side street boundary if the local council won't allow a fence except on the setback line. But do take care you don't create a blind corner for traffic.*

A VANDA — *a garden flower only in the tropics. 'Flowers are the pleasures of the world' (Shakespeare).*

TO DIVIDE SPACE *you can use:*
1 Shrubs — for total separation.
2 Trees — which allow you to see under the branches.
3 Low planting — for a gentle division, maybe with a pergola or roof overhead.
4 A screen fence — or a wall, softened with creepers.
5 & 6 A change of level — with steps as a link, and maybe with planting associated with them.

Indoors and out

Can you move comfortably from the house to the garden? It's not as common as it used to be to find the only door to the back garden is through the laundry, as though we were still living in the days when the only people who went out back were the servants, but do you actually have a door from the family room, and would it be desirable to have one from the kitchen or even a main bedroom? Replacing a window with a door isn't a major job for a builder, and it might allow you to think of stepping out from a living room onto a terrace or deck, maybe into the sunshine, maybe with a pergola overhead for shade. If there is already a patio, is it adequate for your purposes, or should you think of making it more generous? If the ground is flat, you may be able to walk out at the same level as the house; but there is almost always a slope, however slight (you can see it most clearly along the walls of the house) and if the house is one of those old-fashioned ones that sits a little above the ground, steps will be needed. Should they be at the door, or can you build up the terrace to meet it?

If the ground slopes

A sloping site may call for some juggling of earth to create level areas for outdoor living, with banks and maybe retaining walls and steps to link it all together. Here you have another design theme, one that can be so effective that people have been known to create level changes where they weren't really needed, just for interest. But remember that earthworks will mean either money

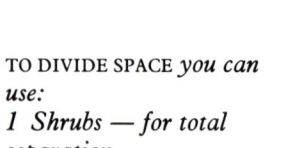

= Designing a garden =

to a contractor or backbreaking work — a level site is easier to develop.

On the other hand, a strongly sloping hillside site might well have fine views, and you will want to ensure that your plants frame them while at the same time masking distractions — which usually take the form of the neighbours' houses and electricity poles. A two-storey house may have views from upstairs too, so make sure the garden looks good from there.

IMAGINATION CAN OFTEN *turn the liabilities of a site into assets. These huge rocks were pushed out of the way by the builder. Far too big to truck away, they have been made the basis of a rockery that sets this front garden (in Canberra) apart from its neighbours. Is the planting just a wee bit fussy, though? Trees and simple shrubs and groundcovers give a more natural appearance (see drawing).*

TREES: NATIVES WOULD BE BEST TO HARMONISE WITH THE ROCKS

PLANTING CARRIED RIGHT UP TO THE FOOTPATH

LUSH SHRUBBERY WITH ROUNDED & SOFTLY-FOLIAGED SHRUBS

ABOVE: *Weeds are a nuisance in an established garden, but a comfort in a new one; if your soil can't grow* them *it won't grow anything!*

God Almighty first planted a garden, and indeed it is the purest of human pleasures, the greatest refreshment for the spirit of man
Francis Bacon

RIGHT: *A steep site, rocky, with hardly any soil, and that thin and sandy — yet there is potential for a magical bushland garden here. As the Japanese say, 'Listen to the land, and it will tell you what it wants to be.'*

FAR RIGHT: *With imagination and love, you can make a garden just about anywhere. This one is on a roof, several floors above a city street.*

Are there trees?
Do you have trees already, either wild — in Australia this usually means eucalypts — or planted? There is nothing that can give the garden a head start like they can, and you should think very carefully indeed before deciding to remove any. Even if a tree is a bit scruffy now, a few years' care will likely see it grow to beauty. Judicious pruning may be needed to reveal handsome trunks and branches. If you have doubts about the safety of any tree, call in expert advice.

Paths and pavements are another matter. If they fit your purposes, fine, but if they don't — and some builders seem to have a genius for putting them in strange places — the cost of replacing them will be well spent.

The soil
What sort of soil do you have to work with? If it's not the ideal deep, crumbly loam, don't worry — beautiful gardens have been made on all soil types. It's almost always better to work with what you have than to import topsoil (unless your builder has carried all your natural topsoil away or buried it irretrievably under subsoil and rubble). Any soil can be improved out of sight by cultivation and the addition of as much organic matter — compost and its like — as you can manage.

Check your drainage — just dig a couple of holes about half a metre deep, fill them up with water, and if it has drained away after twenty-four hours, you have no worries. If it hasn't, you might think of laying agricultural drains, planting in raised beds, or accepting the soil as it is and planting things that like wet feet — there is a wide range to choose from apart from willows.

It's handy to know how much lime your soil has — whether it is alkaline or acid — as there are some desirable plants that don't like the stuff. Generally, soils on the east coast tend to be acid and inland soils are usually alkaline or neutral. If you can wait until Christmas, look at the colour of hydrangeas in your area; if they are blue, the ground is acid, if pink, there is lime about. Alternatively, your local department of agriculture or the parks department of the local council can advise you.

By-laws and regulations
And while you're talking to the council, check to see if they have any regulations and policies that might affect you. They'll likely want to approve any structures you might propose — pergolas, fences, sheds — and might have thoughts on the use of water or the removal of trees.

You'll find, too, that your parks people are a mine of information about the best plants for your area — as are your local nurseries.

Birds in the garden

A long time ago, it is said, a certain emperor of China ordered all the sparrows in the palace gardens killed, his excuse being that their chirping distracted him from affairs of state. The Chinese have never forgiven him, for what crimes might lurk in the breast of a man who could live in a garden where no birds sing?

BIRDS WILL COME, even to city gardens, if they aren't driven away by marauding cats and pesticide-happy gardeners; if you provide the sort of environment they like, some will decide to take up residence. This means planting trees and shrubs for them to roost in, allowing mulch and litter to stay on the ground where worms and insects can be found, and choosing plants which provide the birds with food.

Which plants?
Very many Australian birds eat honey, so nectar-bearing flowers are a must. Think of grevilleas, hakeas and their tribe; of eucalypts; of the Gymea lily. Parrots and others eat seeds, even of such exotic plants as crabapples and cotoneasters; sunflowers too, and tea-trees. Most plants will attract insects and the sort of birds that feed on them.

If all this sounds like a call for native plants, then you read aright; but there is no need to confine yourself to them if you don't want to. Just don't leave them out altogether, especially the eucalypts.

THINK TWICE about removing hollow trees — or even hollow branches — unless they really are unsafe. Many birds use them as nesting places and will happily take up residence.

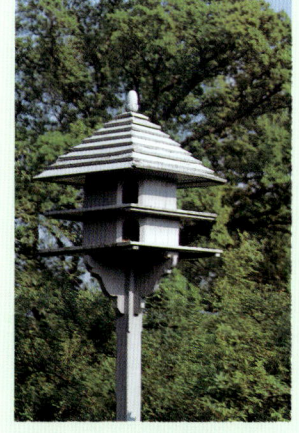

ABOVE: *A splendid birdhouse, attractive enough to be the centrepiece of the garden. Raise it high, out of the reach of cats.*

BELOW LEFT: *A simple concrete dish makes a birdbath and mirrors the sky. Notice how the path curves around it.*

Accessories for birds
If you like, you can provide birdbaths, birdhouses and feeding tables; but don't feed your birds so generously that they become dependent on you. And if the chirruping should distract you from affairs of state? Are there not more important things in life?

ABOVE: *The protea family all provide honey for the birds that pollinate them. This is the* Grevillea 'Ned Kelly'.

LEFT: *Rainbow lorikeets coming to dine at the veranda.*

Working with a designer

While designing and creating a garden is one of life's happier tasks, it's not one that you have to tackle on your own; if you feel you could use help and advice, by all means call in a professional.

GARDEN DESIGNERS come in several breeds: *Landscape Architects*, who are members of the Australian Institute of Landscape Architects (or its fellow in New Zealand) and are bound by its code of ethics, are trained specialists in design. You can expect your LA to have considerable knowledge of horticulture, but also to be able to take a whole and balanced view of your needs — to be as aware of people as of plants and construction. Not all LAs plan gardens (many specialise in parks, commercial properties and the like), but the office of the AILA in your state capital will be able to put you in touch with firms that do. Before you choose a firm, ask to see some examples of its work, so that you can see if its usual style of design suits you. The LA works in much the same way as an architect does, preparing preliminary designs ('sketch plans') for your approval, developing these into 'working' or 'contract' documents, helping in the selection of a contractor, and then monitoring the contractor's work to ensure it is done in accordance with the designs. But you needn't engage him for the complete service if you don't need it. LAs' fees, like architects', have traditionally been based on a percentage of the estimated cost of the project, but many find it fairer on relatively small projects like an average garden, to charge an hourly rate.

Nurseries and contractors

Many of the larger *Nurseries* undertake garden design — talk to your State's Nurserymen's Association for recommendations — sometimes as part of a design-and-construct package, sometimes as a separate service. Charges vary, and you should check before you proceed with a particular firm. Nurserymen are, nowadays, usually trained horticulturists, and are usually knowledgeable on plants and planting design.

Landscape Contractors, who might also call themselves *Landscape Gardeners* or just *Landscapers*, usually offer design as part of a design and build service. You can find them through the Landscape Contractors' Association, or under their various titles in the yellow

ABOVE: *A hybrid* Vanda. *If you want to grow flowers like orchids which need special conditions, alert your designer!*

BOTTOM RIGHT: *Perfect proportions — the signature of a skilled designer. And bold and original use of plants too; these giant daisies flanking the path are Montanoas.*

BELOW: *Aquilegia alpina, a flower for a romantic garden.*

pages (you might look for *Horticultural* or *Garden Consultants* there too). Many of these firms do excellent work, but, regrettably, the industry is plagued by cowboys whose main interest is in selling you the rocks, bark chips, paving blocks and plants they stock. As always, talk to the firm and ask to see examples of its work before you commit yourself, and get the agreed price in writing.

Design-by-post

There are also design–by–post services available; you send them your site plan and some photographs, and for a fairly moderate fee, you get a design, usually including recommended plants. The result can only be as good as the basic information you give, and you should consider how important it is to you that you and your designer meet face to face, and that the designer has first-hand knowledge of your site.

Cost and fees

With any garden designer, of course, you are paying for experience — you have a right to expect that your designer has 'been there' and has learned from his or her mistakes. But don't expect him to read your mind. The partnership is much more likely to be a success if you have a clear idea yourself of just what your needs are and just what it is that you want your designer to do. Be prepared to ask (and to answer) many questions. Two hundred years ago that elegant architect and garden designer, Sir William Chambers, said that half the success of a fine design is owing to a clear-headed and understanding client. This is still true today.

If you have two loaves, sell one and buy a lily
Chinese saying

ABOVE: *It can take courage to be bold — as in this planting of massed irises flanking a dead-straight path. Imagine how much less effective it would be if there was a jumble of shapes and colours.*

LEFT: *The same flowers — irises — used in a small group to accent a doorway. In both contexts, they are just right!*

PUTTING IT ON PAPER

Now that you've made an objective assessment of your needs and your site, it's time to put your plan on paper. As long as you can understand your own doodles, it doesn't matter whether you make them in colour or with a soft lead pencil — try both and see which you find easier. And don't worry if your doodle ends up as a confusing mass of lines and corrections, just lay a piece of tracing paper over it, pick out the lines you want, and continue. Once you've decided which of your doodles you like the most, draw it up on a larger scale using graph paper or make an enlarged photocopy.

Experience is the name everyone gives to his mistakes
Oscar Wilde

On another piece of tracing paper, start to work out your ideas in detail, checking the measurements (is that path wide enough? Is there room for the screening shrubs in that planting area? Should there be steps between the patio and the lawn?) and making sure you haven't forgotten anything important. But resist the temptation to elaborate the design — remember the art of all art is knowing when to stop. It can be amusing to draw in every paving brick, every little plant, and if it helps you to visualise your design, go ahead. But remember the plan is just a means to an end, just a diagram. If you are looking at a detail, say a set of steps, don't waste time drawing the rest of the garden as well — give each detail its own piece of tracing paper and collate them onto your final plan.

Don't make your plans too large or you'll spend forever just drawing lines. A working plan can be 1:100 (the scale to which architects' plans are drawn); your doodles can be half that (1:200) — and if you want to work out things like steps or intricate plantings in detail, 1:50 is adequate.

Think of the third dimension

A plan can be deceptive, it gives an exaggerated emphasis to things like paving patterns, and it flattens out the third dimension of height. We always draw trees and shrubs as circles on plan, but that's not how we see them in real life. You can plot perspective drawings, which will give you a photograph-like impression of how things will look, but perspective needs considerable artistic skill. It's much easier to simply tilt the plan at an angle and draw in the trees and things at their measured height. This gives you a sort of bird's eye view (it is technically known as an 'axonometric projection'), and though the heights tend to look a bit exaggerated, it can be a great help at all stages of making the design.

Getting down to specifics

Now, as you get close to your final layout, you can begin to think in terms of materials and specific plants. Will the patio be brick? concrete? stone? Will those screening shrubs, which you see in your mind's eye as evergreen and two or three metres tall, be camellias? shrub roses? grevilleas? What will those groundcovers be, and will there be spring bulbs among them? Is there a suitable home for some must-have favourite? How will the colours and textures of foliage blend? Ideally, the question should be: what is the best plant for this spot? rather than, where can I put this plant? But it's usually a little of both, and there's no need to try to work out all your planting details on paper — half the fun of gardening is improvising, playing with planting schemes and changing things around, all within the framework that your overall design has created.

Once you've made your final plan — the one you will be referring to as you make the garden — you'll need to make copies, you don't want your precious original falling in the mud. If it's small enough to fit on a photocopy machine, that will be the cheapest way, if not, take it to a plan printers and have the job done there.

ABOVE: *The equipment you need to draw plans is simple: tracing and graph paper, a draughtsman's scale ruler marked in centimetres, maybe some coloured marker pens, a set square and a surveyor's tape measure.*

SITE PLAN

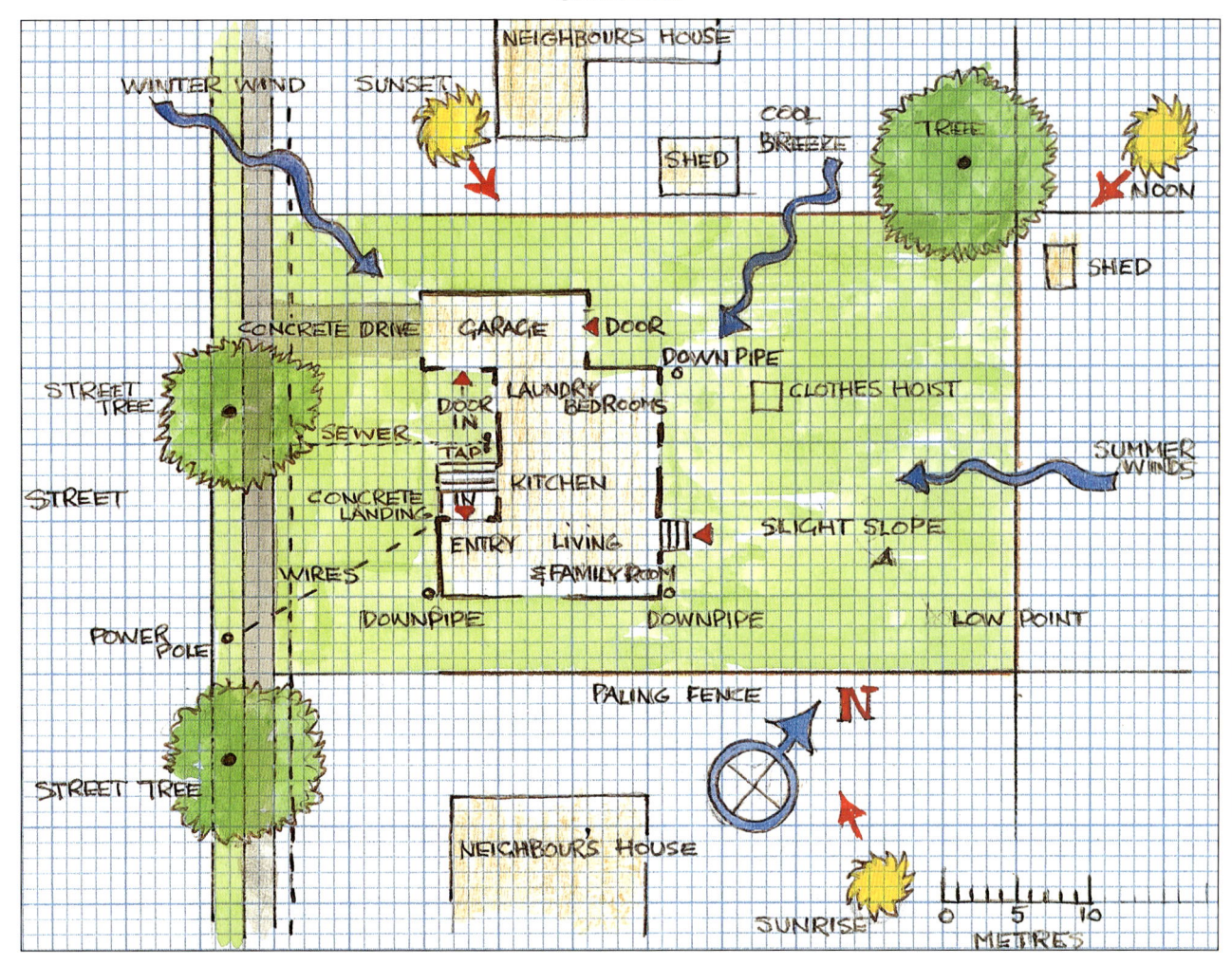

ABOVE: *The first stage in making a design is to assemble a plan of the property as it exists. Architects' and builders' plans can serve as a basis (the local council may have copies if you haven't), but you'll still need to measure fences, trees, sewer lines and such. Show everything that might affect your design. Graph paper helps to keep everything in scale (1:100 is usual).*

SIMPLIFY, SIMPLIFY... *do handsome trees like this really need such a clutter at their feet?*

Landscaping your garden

The Rules of Good Design

Works of art — and beautiful gardens — aren't created from rule books; but there are some general principles that most garden designers would agree on. A successful design is balanced and harmonious, neither so complex that it will seem fussy and overdone in reality, nor so over-simple that it will be boring. (But remember that plants will bring beauty as their birthright, so it's best to err on the side of simplicity.)

Take a look at the doodles on these two pages, based on the site plan on page 17. Which are the more pleasing? (Feel free to scribble notes to yourself on your doodles, and follow your own judgment!) There are more doodles and plans on the following few pages.

ABOVE: *Scented-leaved pelargoniums make splendid groundcovers on even the most unpromising soil.*

BELOW: *At the doodle stage, this multi-coloured planting would have been represented simply by a patch of green, maybe labelled 'low planting'.*

1 *Not very interesting*

2 *A little too equal*

3 *A bit dull*

4 *Also a bit dull*

5 *Garden rooms*

6 *Needs to be simplified*

= Putting it on paper =

7 *An unfinished look*

8 *A more unified design*

9 *An informal planting of trees*

10 *Trees used to enclose a space*

DAINTY FLOWERS *such as fuchsias play a role in the garden like pictures do in a living room — they embellish the main structure.*

DESIGN AND PLANNING CHECKLIST
Have you allowed for/considered:

- summer shade, winter sun
- windbreaks
- blocking undesirable views, privacy
- drying the washing, compost heaps, storage for garden equipment and furniture
- level changes, steps and/or retaining walls, pavements and lawn levels
- lighting
- letterbox, house number
- drainage
- easements, overhead lines, drains and/or sewers
- the width of paths, gates and steps, the size of pavings and patios, the shape of lawns and the ease of mowing
- security, especially for swimming pools
- space for children's games, herbs, vegetables or other special garden projects
- access for the car
- access to the garden during construction and afterwards
- comfortable access to the house
- can you/do you need to build the garden in stages?
- have you allowed enough space for planting, so that plants won't outgrow themselves and need constant cutting back?
- do you need council approval for fences, structures and pools and for planting on the street?

THE BRIGHT COLOURS *of annuals can dominate the garden — but they are ephemeral and the bones of any garden should be permanent trees and shrubs.*

Landscaping your garden

WHERE SHOULD EVERYTHING GO?

THE PROCESS of design is like a cactus, thorny and unfriendly at first sight but beautiful in bloom.

RIGHT: Lay a piece of tracing paper over your site plan (page 17) and you can begin designing by assigning locations to the various activities the garden is to accommodate. Just vaguely at the moment, to ensure you can fit them all in.

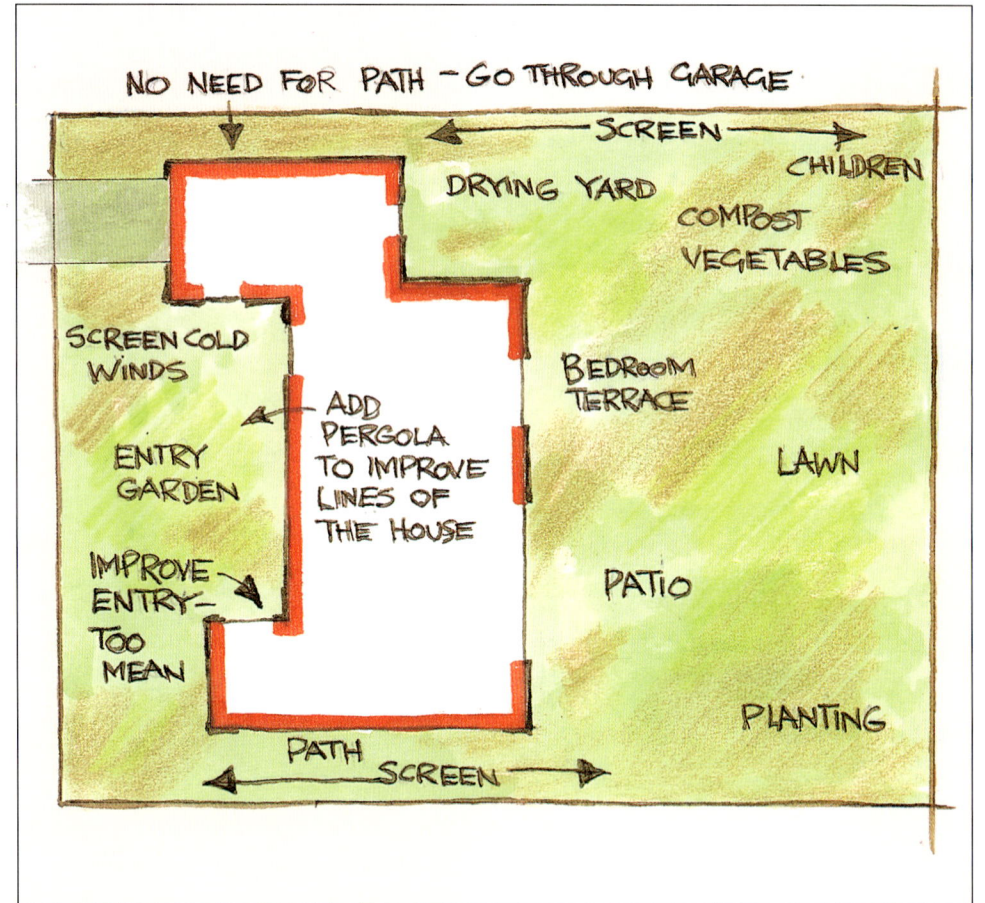

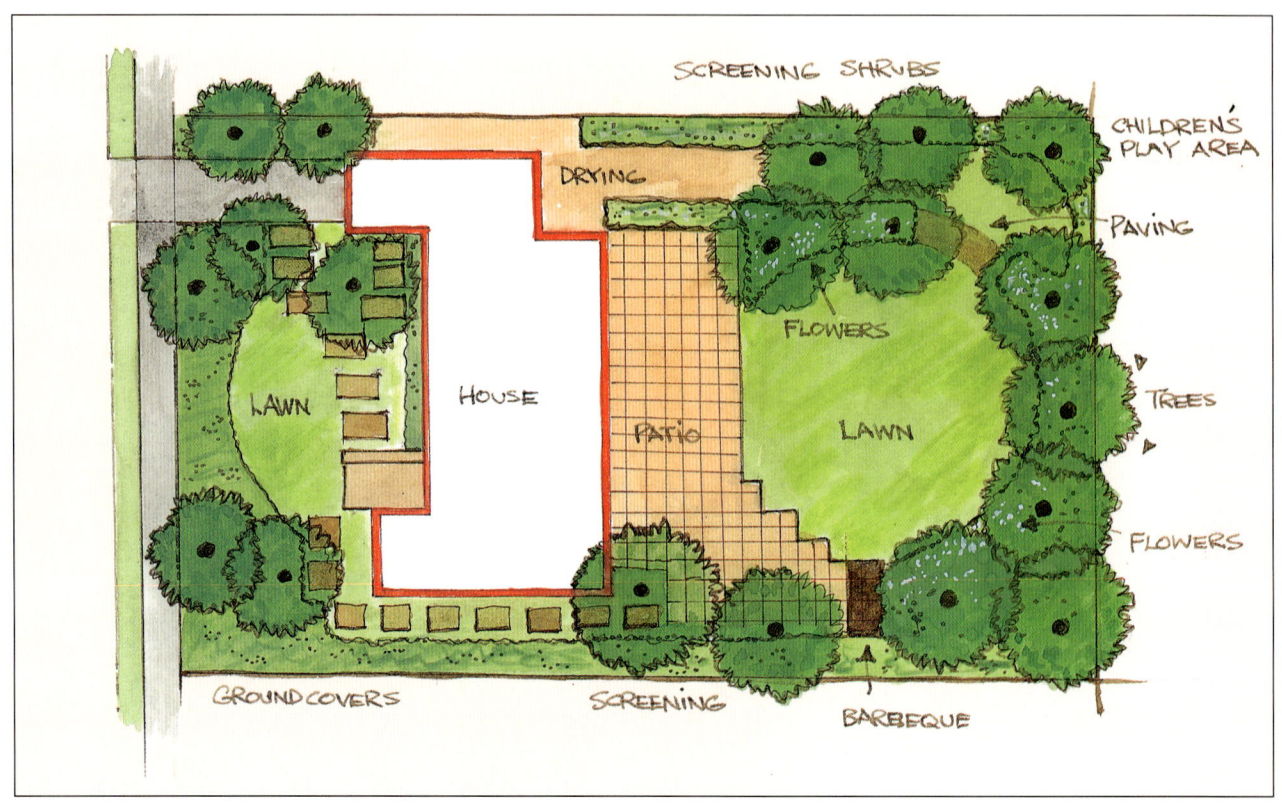

20

= Putting it on paper =

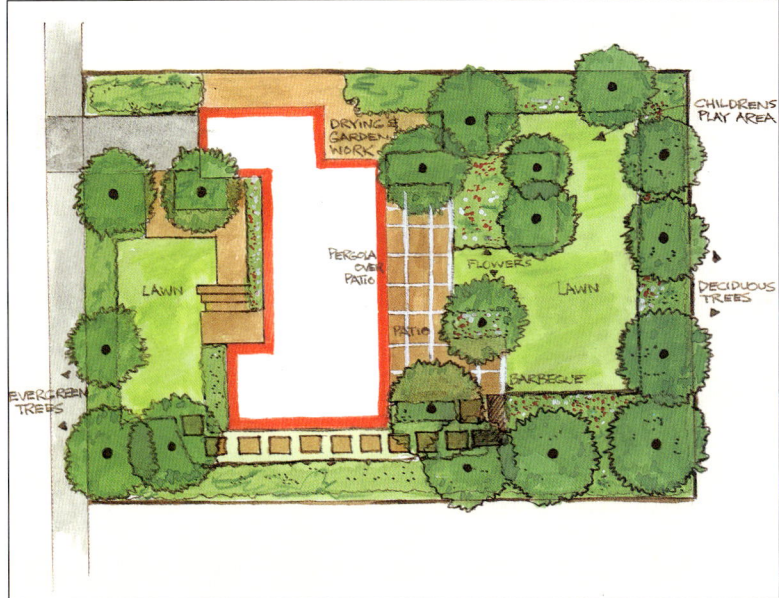

IT ALWAYS HELPS *to have a theme for a design. Here we are doodling with a combination of circles and straight lines (1, opposite), rectangles (2, above right) and triangles (3, below right) based on the site plan on page 17. For a finished design based on the circles, see page 23.*

THE DOODLES *are green — but the garden can still have lots of flower colour in the end, from things like wisteria (above) and impatiens (below). Or it might continue the theme of green like this classic cottage (centre).*

21

Landscaping your garden

ABOVE: *Red petunias,* BELOW LEFT: *Japanese anemones — a fine plant for shaded, slightly moist places and* BELOW RIGHT: *Frangipani (plumeria) a small tree for warm climates.*

A BIRD'S EYE (*axonometric*) view of the circles-and-straight-lines design which helps you to see the third dimension. You make it by simply tipping the plan over at an angle and carrying up your heights to scale.

I walk unseen,
On the dry smooth shaven green
To behold the wandering moon
Milton, Il Penseroso

THE DOODLES HAVE DEVELOPED INTO A DESIGN

Making doodles on a small scale with magic marker, crayons or whatever suits you best, is the heart of the design process — if it doesn't look good in a small doodle, it won't when it's built — but don't get hung up if a doodle doesn't come out right. Chuck it out — paper's cheap enough — go and have a cup of coffee or sleep on it, and try another. There's nothing to be gained by being in a hurry; sooner or later you'll come up with an idea that seems to incorporate all the things you want and which looks promising.

Then you can lay a piece of tracing paper over your original site plan and transfer the doodle idea to it. Now is the time for accuracy, to make sure the paths are wide enough, that the patio is adequate, that there is room for that row of shrubs. The result might look like this one, based on the circle theme from page 20. You still have a lot of pleasant choices to make — what kind of trees? will the patio be brick, concrete or whatever? but you now have a design to provide a framework for your thinking.

How much detail you add to your plan from here on is up to you — a professional designer might want to show everything down to the most intricate details of the planting, but you needn't — it's your garden.

The finished design, based on the circles design on page 20 and traced onto graph paper.

Getting it on the ground

Having made your plans, how do you set about turning them into a garden? The de-luxe way is to hire a contractor to do it all, from the initial earthworks to the final planting, and there are advantages in this.

YOU CAN ALWAYS ADD *touches to a garden; the sculptured tortoise would have looked lonely if it had been placed before the plants grew up.*

B*ut you should have seen my garden last week...*
Ruth Draper

IT SAVES YOU TIME and a lot of hard work of course; a contractor probably knows more people in the business than you do, and he may well be able to find plants and materials more easily than you can; you can expect a high standard of workmanship; and once the contract has been signed, you have a clear picture of what it will all cost (but budget for another 10 per cent or so for the unforeseen extras that always seem to come up).

Naturally, this is the most expensive way, and you can save money by having the contractor only take the project part of the way and finishing it off yourself. There is a lot to be said for having him carry out the heavy work (earthworks, grading, drainage, maybe structures like pergolas and at least the major paving), reserving the less arduous tasks of planting for yourself. If one of your contractor's men does his back in or drops a slab of concrete on his toes, he will be covered by worker's compensation, and it's the contractor's problem. But if it's *you* laid up for days or weeks, let alone a friend who's offered to lend a hand.... And can you really face a run of weekends hauling dirt and bricks?

Working with a contractor
Let us say you decide to call in a contractor, either for the whole job or part of it. How do you find one? If you've used a landscape architect to design the garden, he will be able to make a recommendation; if you're building (or altering) the house, the builder may be able to take on the garden as part of his job (he'll probably sub-contract at least the planting part); you can look in the yellow pages; talk to your local landscape contractors' association; or advertise, yourself, for tenders in the local paper. Whichever, it is well worth getting at least three quotes. Prices for landscape work vary more than in any other section of the building industry, and it is not at all uncommon to find your highest price more than double the lowest.

It's courteous to tell each prospective contractor that you're seeking other tenders, but you're not obliged to tell him from whom. You're entitled to ask to see some examples of his work (and to ask the owners about his performance), and for assurance of his solvency — a contractor going bankrupt in the middle of a job is a real nightmare.

Getting quotes
Make sure you get your quotes in writing, and that you understand what each includes. If you're contracting for the complete job, you may find included a 'maintenance' or 'establishment' period. This doesn't mean you'll be getting a full-time gardener for the period — usually three or six months — but you can expect the contractor to visit the finished job from time to time to give the new plantings and grass the basic after-care they need to establish properly. It's rather like the after-sales service you get when you buy a car, and if you are confident in your ability to look after the new plantings, you can save money by not including it. Ask.

Once you've accepted a price (usually the lowest, of course) you have a contract and work can start. But do confirm it in writing; and make sure you're clear whether you will be paying at the end or in a series of progress payments, and at what stages they are due. And check with the tax department whether you will be obliged to deduct tax from the payments and, if so, how to do it.

Be decisive
Ask any contractor and he'll tell you his pet hate is a customer who can't make up his mind what he wants. If you gave him drawings (no matter how sketchy)

Getting it on the ground

THE MAKING OF A GARDEN OVER THREE YEARS

Year 1
- Major earthworks (by a contractor?)
- Fences
- Main paths and driveways (so that you can get into the house unmuddied)
- Set out the patio, either planting it with grass or laying gravel as a temporary surface which will serve as the base for paving later
- Trees. No one ever does this one, and everyone realises later that had they done so, they would be enjoying the shade by now
- Grass, which could be left to year 2 and a green manure crop (clover, potatoes, or lucerne) planted this year to improve the soil
- Green manure or holding crop (nasturtiums etc) on future planting areas

Year 2
- Retaining walls, steps, lawn, prepare planting beds
- Patio (a first stage, perhaps)
- Pergola framework, with the vines planted at the base (the joists can come now or next year)
- Set out planting areas, plant major shrubs

Year 3
- Finish patio and pergola
- Finish plantings, groundcovers
- Ornaments (sculpture etc)

ON THE NEXT THREE PAGES, we follow the building of a terrace house garden from beginning to end.

This page, top to bottom:

1 Looking from an upstairs window down the length of the garden. The ground slopes uncomfortably; making a series of levels connected by single steps will allow for places to sit.

2 The garden looks like a disaster area — but things are happening — soil is being levelled, bricks being put in place. The fate of the odd lot of ill-chosen plants left by previous owners is still to be decided.

3 Just below the house, the main change of level has been established and steps built.

4 Right at the bottom of the garden — dirt and junk. If it were a bigger place, this area could be left for a second stage, after the part next to the house was finished.

The following pages show the garden in more advanced stages.

HIPPEASTRUMS *are spectacular bulbs for mild climates — just one or two brings a splash of scarlet to a small garden.*

to work from, you will have got off to a good start, but as the design takes shape on the ground it is easy to be prey to second thoughts. Do resist them, and if your man asks you questions, give him a definite answer. He'll often have suggestions about how best to do things: don't be afraid to ask if they will involve extra cost. And always talk to the man himself; he won't be doing everything, and it can cause much confusion if you leave instructions with his sub-contractor. Remember, he is as keen as you are that his work will do credit to you both.

Timetables

If you decide to do the lion's share of the work yourself, the first question is whether to do it all at once or spread it out over two or three years. Spreading the work has the double advantage of making it easier to pay for and allowing you some weekends for something other than garden building; but the scope of the job comes into it too. A tiny city yard, calling only for paving that can be laid in a couple of weekends and a few plants to follow, might be best tackled in a single campaign; a larger suburban garden, with pavings, maybe a pergola, and more extensive plantings may well be better staged over three or four years.

The contractor, for whom time is money, usually organises his job something like this:

1 *Earthworks* Any major ground shaping that needs machinery (he might take down a section of the fence for access), followed at once by any drains that have to be laid.

2 *Rough carpentry* Formwork for concrete, timber retaining walls and the like.

3 *Masonry* Pavings, retaining walls, driveways.

4 *Large trees* Advanced trees that need to be moved by trucks.

5 *Fine carpentry* Fences (if they're not there already), pergolas, seats and what have you.

6 *Topsoil and fine grading of planting beds and lawns* Watering systems usually go in at this stage, garden lighting too (lines that run beneath pavements

THE GAP BETWEEN *the back of the house and the fence has been covered with a pergola for shade and comfort; the built-in seats and coffee table (an outdoor livingroom indeed!) are a nice touch. Soon vines will grow on the walls to soften the severe lines.*

BELOW THE MAIN STEPS, *the line of the brick paving becomes more informal. A couple of the existing trees have been kept and augmented with new plantings. With greater care than formerly, the garden will leaf out quite quickly.*

Getting it on the ground

will have been laid at paving time).
7 Planting and grassing
This arrangement avoids going over completed work as much as possible, but if you're staging over a period you can't always follow it exactly; but you should try to avoid the upset of finding that you have to pull out plantings to get a load of bricks in or adjust some levels.

An in-ground swimming pool is a big construction, and best done as early as possible; but it's also a big expense, and may have to be put off until after year 3. In the meantime, its site could be grass or gravel, and you will be taking care not to put any permanent features across the future contractor's access.

Tread carefully
Most people rush in with the grass first of all, and then find themselves doing a lot of digging and cursing as they try to get rid of bits of it, or find themselves having to repair the damage caused by loads of pavers trundled over it. Sowing the rough-graded area to clover may not be orthodox, but it works; the clover gives you a cover against dust, and is dug in at lawn-preparation time to the great benefit of the grass or other plantings.

This sequence isn't carved on tablets of stone. If you find it needs adjusting to suit your priorities, go ahead, but when you've worked out your programme, try to keep to it.

TOP RIGHT: *Looking back towards the house after a couple of years' growth. The trees and shrubs are lush and shady, the brick paving is beginning to mellow.*

BOTTOM RIGHT: *From the house the garden looks much bigger than it is — you look through the pergola-roofed living and dining space to lushness and green beyond.*

DESIGN FOR THE CLIMATE

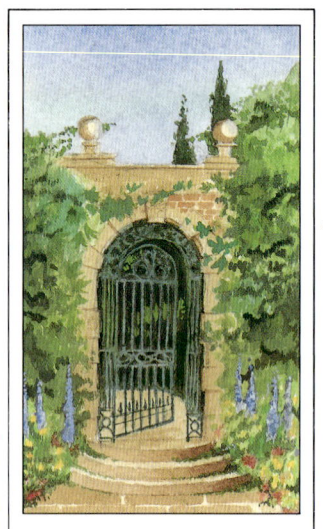

It's always pleasant to sit in the sun in winter, and often in autumn and spring too. In summer, however, a retreat to the shade is in order — unless of course you're cultivating your suntan.

A comfortable garden needs a balance between sun and shade, through the day and through the year, and once you know which way your property faces — where north is — you can plan for it quite easily.

M*ake no mean little plans*
Gianlorenzo Bernini

TREES ON THE NORTH SIDE *to shade the house and the patio. This is* Delonix regia, *the royal poinciana.*

We all know of course that the sun rises in the east, sets in the west, and is at its highest at noon, when, except in the tropics, it's never quite overhead but somewhere to the north. This is why the north side of the house gets the sun and the south side is in its own shade for most of the year. But not in summer, because the summer sunrise and sunset are quite a bit to the south of an east-west line. This means that at midsummer the hot afternoon sun will hit your 'shady' south side patio at about three o'clock and stay there for the rest of the day, upsetting any shade-loving plants growing there. Unshaded pavement will heat up like a Dutch oven and radiate heat into the house long after sunset.

The ideal aspect

Conversely, the winter sun moves to the north and doesn't rise so high; shadows are longer, and that spot you chose in December for the vegetable garden because it was so sunny, may turn out to get no winter sun at all and precious little in autumn and spring.

The ideal aspect for outdoor living is the north or north-east side of the house, where the winter sun is assured. An area of pavement here can reflect its

= Design for the climate =

warmth to the house, but you'll need to provide shade for the summer. You could rig up awnings or sun umbrellas — and very pretty they can look, too — but the shade of trees is cooler (the constant transpiration of water from their leaves acts as a natural air-conditioner). Deciduous trees let the winter sun through their bare branches; plant them on the east for the early winter sun. Evergreens can go to the south, and maybe on the west also, as in our hot climate the afternoon sun is rarely welcome.

NO VERANDA *is able to keep out the afternoon sun which just shines straight under it. An awning of vines (trained on one or two wires) provides a solution. Cooler than canvas too, both because it lets any breeze in and doesn't trap hot air, and because transpiration from the leaves cools the air among them.*

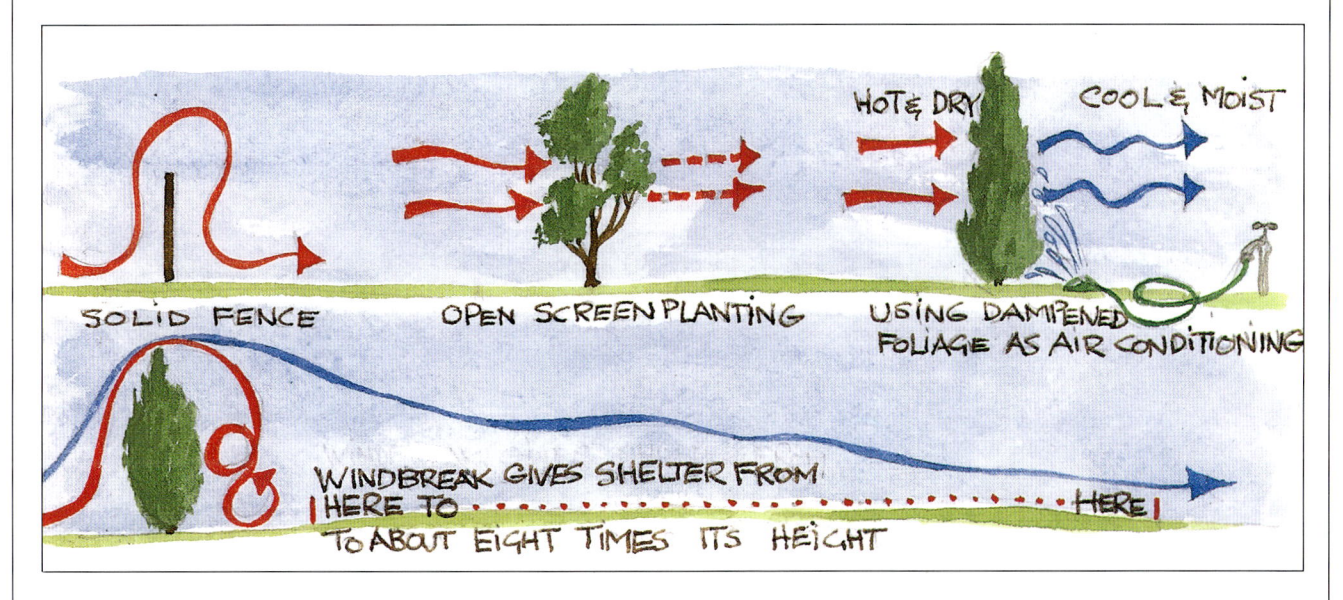

Shading the house

Tall trees shading the roof can make quite a difference to your comfort inside, and large areas of glass cry out for shade. Remember, once the sun gets into your rooms, it's reluctant to leave. If shade trees will dominate the garden too much don't forget the ancient climate-control device of the vine-covered pergola. Pergolas needn't always be attached to the house but can wander about the garden too.

TOP: *Controlling the wind.* BOTTOM: *Sun and shade change as the sun moves with the seasons.*

IT'S PROBABLY better to err on the side of too much shade than too little; most trees will put up with a bit of judicious pruning and thinning if they get too dense.

29

A Temperate Climate Garden

In Melbourne's temperate (but sometimes capricious) climate, this garden follows to the letter the rules of design for year-round comfort yet it is by no means stereotyped in its design. There are paved areas against the north side of the house, with deciduous trees to shade them in summer and let in the winter sun.

A brick patio provides, in quite a small garden, a choice of places to sit. A path in matching brick curves from it to another small paved area at the top of the garden, screened by shrubs so that it is not seen from the house. By taking an indirect route, the path distracts the eye from the narrowness of the site, and the cunning placement of granite boulders gives point to its curves — we accept the idea that the path *had* to weave around them. On a larger scale, trees or dense shrubbery would perform the same trick.

The pictures were taken in midwinter, and you can see the emphasis on evergreen shrubs, which provide year-round privacy.

A CORNER *of the patio, where a small fountain (top) splashes in the shade. The bricks, laid herringbone fashion, match those of the house. They would have looked frighteningly red when they were new, but they have mellowed with a few years' weathering. The terracotta pots match too.*

LOOKING DOWN *the length of the garden from the top patio. The lawn, mainly of shade-tolerant bents and fescues, is tiny, but it serves to set the patios apart from the main garden; try imagining it replaced with bricks. A change of floor like this can be sufficient to demarcate one 'garden room' from another. The screen plantings are mainly camellias, which enjoy the shade of the trees and provide winter flowers. The rounded shrubs in the foreground match the shapes of the rocks, an idea taken from Japanese gardens. Here they are box, but hebes or kurume azaleas would do the job too.*

THE PLANTINGS *in the Melbourne garden are all of shade loving species, selected as much for their variety of foliage as for their flowers. The sawtoothed brick edging to the lawn was a popular Victorian way to trim a planting bed.*

A MINIMALLY-WATERED *lawn like this does get a little patchy in summer — but does it matter when there's so much else to look at? The orange flowers in the foreground are Californian poppies, which seed themselves around the garden and flower all summer.*

A Dry Climate

South Australia's southern vales are hardly desert — the climate is kind enough to grow some of the world's finest wine grapes — but it is hard country for gardens. The rainfall is only about 500 mm, less than half that of Sydney or Melbourne, and falls mostly during the short winter. Summer can be virtually rainless, with temperatures over 35°C for days on end, and searing north winds that dry the garden out as you watch — conditions familiar all over inland Australia.

Three years ago, this lush and flowery garden (at right) was a paddock for sheep. Faced with the need to conserve precious water — the only supply comes from rainwater tanks and a dam — the owners decided to go with the climate rather than fight it.

Going with the climate
The first decision was to confine their gardening to a manageable area immediately around the house, leaving much of the property under rough grass. The traditional eucalypts and Aleppo pines of the district were planted as windbreaks. The rough grass is left un-

WHEN THE TREES *grow up, they will frame and shelter the house and frame the view.*

To see the world in a grain of sand
And heaven in a wild flower
William Blake

THE FLOWERS *are allowed to spill over the gravel paths; no worries about trimming edges here. Its neutral colour and the dull greens of the native shrubs make a quiet foil to the brilliant flowers — geraniums, daisies and herbaceous perennials.*

watered but cut a couple of times a year both to reduce fire hazard and to provide material for the compost heap; when the trees grow these areas will be pleasant spots for picnic lunches and for the children to play.

The house sits on top of a hill (the views over the vineyards to the sea are stunning) and the garden is laid out in the time-honoured way for high and windswept places, with banks of trees and shrubs forming sheltered enclaves. These are mostly natives from all over Australia, chosen for their ability to flourish without being watered, and they form a soft backdrop for an astonishing range of flowers from dry-summer climates all over the world.

Large areas — wide paths and level sitting places — are surfaced in pea gravel; thirsty lawns are kept to a minimum. Of course, some watering has to be done; even with grass chosen for the region, the lawn needs help in summer, as do many of the flowers, but it is concentrated where it does the most good.

A SUBTROPICAL GARDEN

In the tropics, Sir Noel Coward claimed, only mad dogs and Englishmen go out in the mid-day sun. He was being facetious of course, but it's true that in a hot climate the greatest comfort a garden can offer is cool shade.

A shady garden

This Brisbane garden offers it in abundance, for it is almost completely canopied with trees. But it isn't at all gloomy; the owner has taken care to include among the denser trees, those with lacy foliage whose shade is shot with sunlight. Nor is it always a composition in green; in spring the Flamboyant tree (*Delonix regia*) and the Indian laburnum put on a display of flowers that no cool-climate plants can match, set off against the unchanging green of native trees — eucalypts and palms. Beneath them, a wide variety of shrubs and foliage plants grow; paths are mostly covered with fallen leaves, and there is a little artificial creek — just a long pond — 'flowing' from one side of the back garden to the other. Always interesting, it is a garden that needs surprisingly little maintenance; most of the plants take care of themselves, their roots kept cool by the perpetual mulch of fallen leaves.

THE BRICK PATH *winds through the trees to the front door, separated from the driveway (just out of the picture on the left) by a dense planting. Cycads and native violets flourish in the shade.*

TWO BROAD PLANKS *make a bridge over the creek and lead to the extreme back of the garden, which is dominated by a stilt-rooted* Pandanus *tree. This is the sunniest part of the garden, and the groundcover is roughly-mown grass, which has, so far, shown no inclination to spread into the shady areas. 'Definitely not a lawn!' the owner says.*

THE L-SHAPED *house encloses a shady patio for outdoor dining.*

Saving water

Making a garden forces us to look to the future. For it takes time for a garden to come into its beauty, for trees and shrubs to grow, for walls and pavings to mellow.

WE ALL KNOW that Australia is the driest continent on earth, that we should do our bit to save water, and that the water that we use on our gardens is putting pressure on a very limited and precious resource. But it's so easy to forget, when all we have to do is turn on a tap — until the water bill arrives, that is. Many water supply authorities are already trying to encourage conservation by cutting back on the amount of water a household can use before being presented with an excess water bill; and many experts are warning that our cities could face drastic water shortages within twenty years. Twenty years may seem forever, but it's a short time in the life of a garden; we need to be making water-thrifty gardens *today*.

Sure, water-thriftiness is largely a matter of good management — of mulching, of getting rid of weeds which are great robbers of water, of learning to water plants only when they need it, and then giving them a thorough soaking.

Design contributes to water-thriftiness

Lawns, it has been estimated, take nearly 90 per cent of the water consumed by gardeners — and much of this is wasted — so you might think of either eliminating them altogether from your design or at least ensuring that they are no larger than you really need. Pavements can be arranged so that they drain into adjacent planted areas, rather than into grates and gullies connected with the stormwater system. A surprising amount of water seeps back into the ground through the joints of materials like bricks and concrete cobblestones. Nearby trees will benefit from this.

Collect rainwater

You might consider installing tanks to collect rainwater from the roof, standard practice in country areas and in places like Adelaide where the town water isn't very good — and rainwater is much more pleasant for drinking and washing your hair, too.

FACED WITH HAVING *to carry watering cans in our dry climate, early Australian gardeners were quick to appreciate the beauty of arid-climate plants like the aloes and their relatives, displayed here in a modern planting. Massed like more conventional plants, they give flowers for months and interesting foliage all year.*

MAKING LAVISH USE *of plants from the Mediterranean, South Africa and Australia, the garden on these two pages was designed to be as lush as possible in a dry climate.*

THE GARDEN *is full of varied textures, colours and scents, and the effect is as lush as any gardener could desire — no sand-and-gravel desert garden, this one.*

Saving water

Choose drought-resistant plants

Anyone who has had the distressing experience of watching favourite plants die during drought — or has had to replan a holiday for the lack of a friendly neighbour to water the garden — will know the wisdom of concentrating on plants that can get by with the local rainfall. This needn't cramp your style if you keep the *purpose* of the plants in mind, rather than deciding that you *must* have some particular species. A drought-resistant shrub will give privacy, and a tough groundcover will carpet the ground just as well as a tender one; and you can always put the thirsty beauties, in small numbers, in favoured places where you pass frequently. Near the front door or next to the patio perhaps.

Be especially careful choosing trees. A young tree will be able to benefit from the water you give it, but as it matures its roots will go wider and deeper than the hose can reach; and if it needs a wetter climate than yours it will suffer in drought. Even if it doesn't actually die — and the loss of a cherished tree is a disaster — its beauty will be spoilt and its life will be shortened.

You need local knowledge

This is a big country, with many different climates; when choosing plants your only sure guide is local experience. It is often said that native plants are reliable, as they are born to the country, but if a native comes from a place wetter than yours, it will need assistance. And *no* plant can be called drought-resistant until it is established. Baby plants, even the local natives, need watering; and while you may be planning to throw your hose away in time, you'll need it for the first two or three years of your garden's life at least.

A DETAIL *of the planting. The owners are fond of strong colours and blend them well; the garden scintillates in the summer sunshine.*

ABOVE LEFT: *Everlastings* (Helichrysum) *are one of the most drought-resistant of annuals. They should be — they come from inland Australia.*

TOP LEFT: *Marguerites and dianthus spill over a heavy timber retaining wall. They need some extra water to keep them flowering through a dry summer, but the garden takes much less water than a conventional one of lawns and flowers.*

BOTTOM LEFT: *The ruggedness of railways sleepers matches the weight of stone; and all is softened by sweet alice that seeds itself in the gaps.*

FRONT GARDENS

The first duty of a front garden is to ensure that you and your visitors have a pleasant trip from the street to your front door. Nothing is more annoying than to have to negotiate an obstacle course of wet grass, overhanging foliage and awkwardly designed steps, especially if, as is surprisingly often the case, it's not obvious how to find the front door in the first place.

Build your design around generous, well-lit paths, preferably not leading right under your windows, not forgetting your own route from the garage into the house; and all focusing on the front door. At the door itself, you need adequate space for a small group to wait for you to answer the bell and to gather for their goodbyes afterwards; it's surprising how much comfort can be gained here by even an extra square metre or two of paving. You might even like to think of an entrance patio, especially if this aspect of the house is a comfortable one for outdoor living.

How much privacy?
The problem is that the front can never

TOWN HOUSE DEVELOPMENTS *tend to give you only a flowerbed-sized front garden, often facing a drive or carpark. This one is simply filled with an assortment of perennial flowers — a quick return for a small investment on a rented property.*

A SMALL, *fenceless front garden to a modern house. The steps and the simply-designed letterbox mark the boundary, and the path curves across the nature strip to meet the driveway at the kerb. Planting is an assortment of easy-care groundcovers and small trees and shrubs.*

= Front gardens =

be totally private — there's always the chance of being interrupted by a door-to-door survey taker or the proverbial neighbour borrowing a cup of sugar.

How much privacy from the street you'll want is a matter of temperament, though most of us are rather less happy about exposing our homes to the public gaze than our grandparents were. Even in neighbourhoods where front fences are frowned on (do consult your council if you want to build one) judicious use of trees and shrubs, even hedges, will take away the wide-open feeling; they can be augmented with panels of groundcovers if you don't feel like maintaining the usual front lawn.

*A garden is not made
By singing 'O how beautiful!'
And sitting in the shade*
Kipling

WHERE THERE ARE NO FENCES, *the driveways are often the apparent boundaries. If you can co-operate with your neighbours to match up your plantings on either side of the (imaginary) boundary, you all gain a feeling of greater space, and the appearance of the whole street benefits.*

BEFORE: *There's nothing much wrong with this garden in a street without front fences — it's just dull. The fine tree is an asset, but the conifer next to the front door is ill-chosen. It will be blotting out the living room window before too long.*

AFTER: *It hasn't taken much to lift the whole effect. A little stone paving along the drive, not really wide enough to be a path, invites people to walk there and relieves the hard straight line of the concrete. The conifer has been replaced with lower-growing evergreens, and a sweep of flowers (they might be impatiens, madagascar periwinkles [Catharanthus] or even gazanias) decorates the route to the front door. The flower display also keeps visitors from short-cutting across the front lawn, and eliminates the awkward bit of mowing at the base of the big tree. Two new small trees (crepe myrtles, flowering plums or bauhinias would be nice) are placed strategically; one to frame the front door and one to lightly screen the white house on the right. A third could be added at the left to mask the plain end wall of the house and complete the framing.*

Landscaping your garden

IF YOU'RE PLANNING *off-street parking for your guests you need to consider the layout very carefully to ensure that there is room for cars to get in and out without bumping into each other. And it will be a test of skill to keep the front garden from looking like the entrance to a supermarket. Lavish plantings help, and so does a good-quality paving — cars don't* have *to drive on asphalt.*

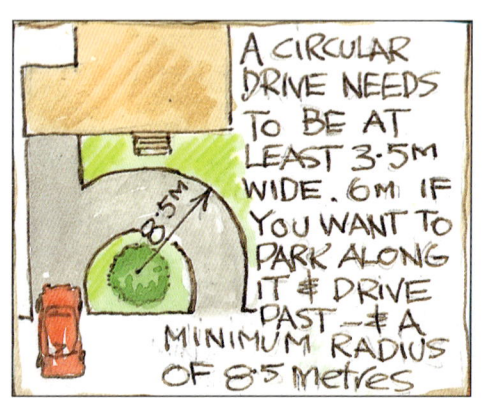

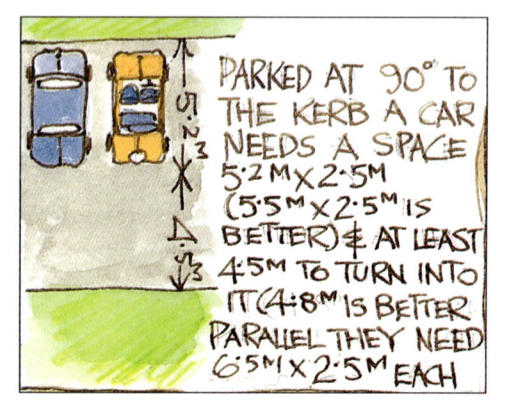

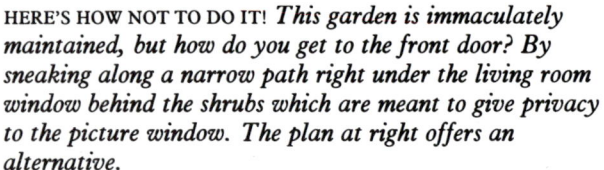

ALLOW THIS MUCH SPACE FOR THE CARS THEMSELVES

ANGLE PARKING ALONG A DRIVE CALLS FOR A MINIMUM WIDTH OF 7.6 METRES — 8 METRES IS BETTER

A CIRCULAR DRIVE NEEDS TO BE AT LEAST 3.5M WIDE. 6M IF YOU WANT TO PARK ALONG IT & DRIVE PAST — & A MINIMUM RADIUS OF 8.5 METRES

PARKED AT 90° TO THE KERB A CAR NEEDS A SPACE 5.2M X 2.5M (5.5M X 2.5M IS BETTER) & AT LEAST 4.5M TO TURN INTO IT (4.8M IS BETTER PARALLEL THEY NEED 6.5M X 2.5M EACH

HERE'S HOW NOT TO DO IT! *This garden is immaculately maintained, but how do you get to the front door? By sneaking along a narrow path right under the living room window behind the shrubs which are meant to give privacy to the picture window. The plan at right offers an alternative.*

A PATH *striking out across the lawn now leads to the front door, and trees and groundcovers fill the triangular space between it and the drive. A path could remain under the window. The trees need not be forest giants; small eucalypts like* Eucalyptus scoparia, *birches, or koelreuterias (golden rain trees) would be suitable.*

Front gardens

A DENSE AND PRIVATE *planting of trees and shrubs, mainly native, clothes the slope in front of this house in Brisbane. Informal steps lead up to the front door past a lattice-screened deck.*

A BIAS towards low-maintenance design is appropriate in the front garden. You don't want to let the neighbourhood down, but then you probably won't want to spend a major proportion of your gardening time keeping the place at its Sunday best for the pleasure of passers-by.

*Ah yet e'er I descend to the grave,
May I a small house and a large garden have!*
Abraham Cowley

TERRACE HOUSE FRONT GARDENS

There is rarely any problem in *planning* the front garden of a terrace house. If there is a garden at all, it is usually only a narrow space between the verandah and the street. What is important is how you treat it in detail; you don't want to spoil the architectural uniformity of the terrace with an inappropriate fence.

Whether you go for timber pickets or cast iron ones depends both on the terrace itself and what the neighbours have, but one or the other is usual, and it always looks best if you and the neighbours paint your fences to match. Then it is only a matter of filling in the space left over from the front path with flowers or greenery as you please.

Adorning the facade with climbing plants can be charming, but if you have iron lace, do keep the climbers dainty — wisteria or *Solandra nitida* with their thick stems are not only out of scale, they can damage the lace, which is surprisingly brittle.

TOWNHOUSE DEVELOPMENTS *often offer little opportunity for a distinctive entry garden, and the simplest treatment is usually the most effective. Here the door is framed on the left by a bottle-brush, which will be trained into a small tree, and by long-flowering daylilies. A restrained creeper could grow over the little pergola to soften the architectural lines still further and provide shade.*

STREETSIDES AND NATURE STRIPS

In most parts of the country, the nature strip, footpath, kerbside verge, call it what you will, is looked after by the person whose property it fronts — and that means you. Since you are spending gardening time there anyway, why not carry the theme of the front garden out to the kerb? It may be simply a matter of letting your grass sweep out without a fence; or your design might be more elaborate.

Consider the public

Three things to remember: the strip of land is the property of the local council, who may need to approve your scheme (particularly if you're thinking of planting trees); you have no real control over marauding children and their dogs, so your plants need to be tough and able to take rough treatment; and the safety of the public has to be considered — *no pricklies like roses or yuccas please*, and take care with groundcovers whose trails might trip people.

ON A WIDE, *and fairly quiet, suburban footpath, gardening spills out in the form of beds of annuals. They prettify the street, and give their owner an excuse to chat to passers-by; few people can resist stopping to admire.*

WHEN A CITY HOUSE *sits right on the footpath — 'bald' in real estate jargon — it can benefit greatly from just a couple of pot plants or a window box. If all the neighbours get together as in this inner-Sydney street, the effect can be magic. So what if you can't walk on the footpaths? There's hardly any traffic here anyway. On a busier street the scope for decorating would be less, and on any street you will have to consider the comfort of the general public.*

OPPOSITE: *The path is just the usual concrete strip, but rather than spend the time mowing the ribbon of grass between it and the kerb, the householder decided she'd have more fun — and give the public more pleasure — with flowers. They're all easy annuals: Californian poppies, a few daisies and larkspurs, boosted with geraniums. None needs a lot of water, so the hose only has to be carted out into the street occasionally.*

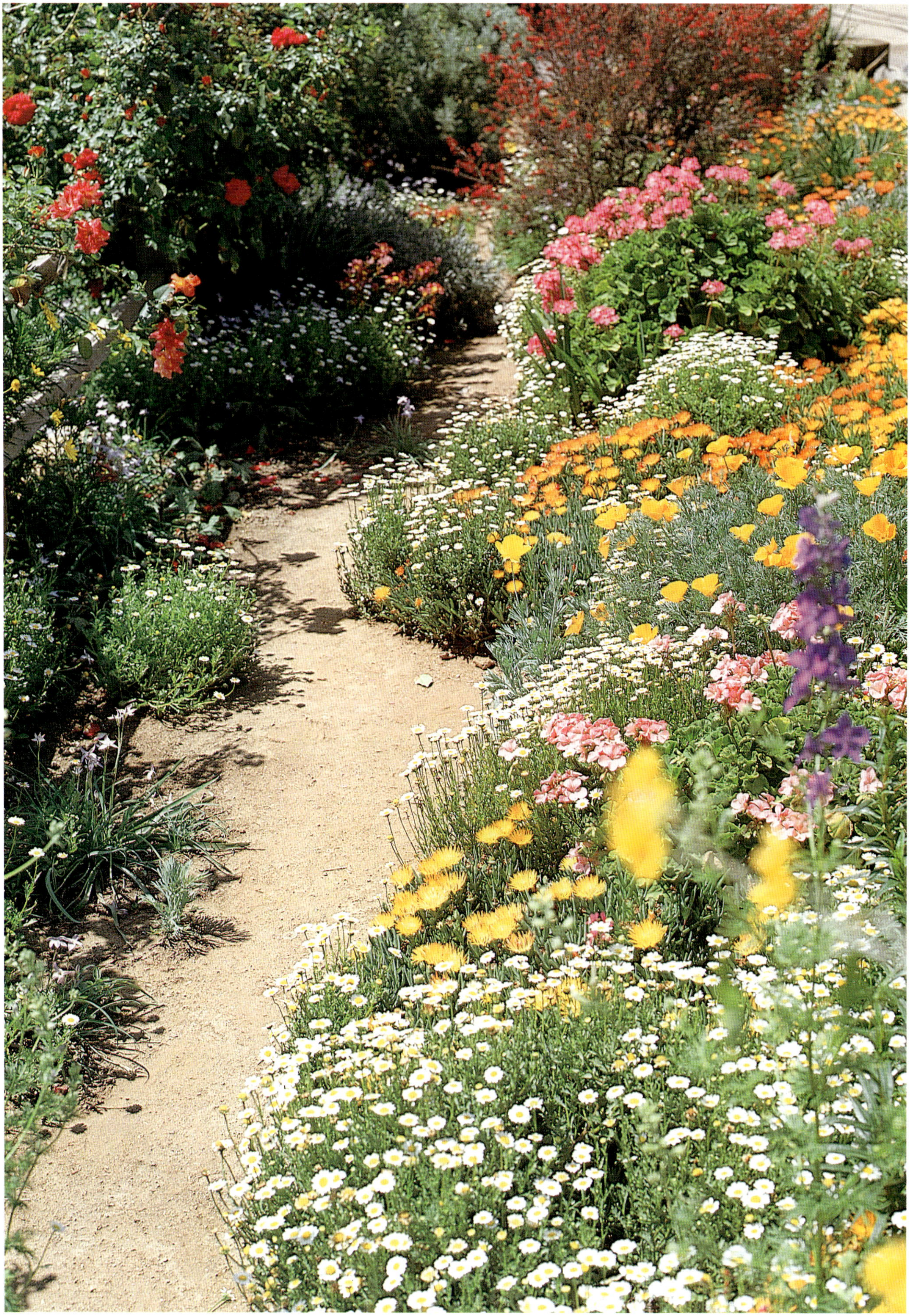

Australian gardens

The story of gardens in Australia really begins in 1788 with the arrival of the first European settlers, for although the Aboriginal people had already lived here for thousands of years and many of the legends of the Dreamtime attest to their appreciation of plants and flowers, they had seen no need to make gardens.

AN OLD-FASHIONED *rose, such as the pioneers adored. They often survive in abandoned gardens.*

IN THE EARLIEST DAYS of settlement, the colonists' most pressing need was for food, and everyone, even the Governor, tried to grow some of his own. This was the beginning of the tradition of the backyard fruit tree that has persisted to this day. Fruits such as oranges and peaches, luxuries back home, flourished in the new land; and as soon as space could be spared from cabbages and beans people started to grow the flowers that reminded them of home. It wasn't long before visitors to the colonies would write admiringly of neat gardens filled with China roses and geraniums, with marigolds and pansies, mixed together in the simple manner we still call 'cottage gardening', and reflecting the symmetry and plainness of colonial architecture.

THE HERBACEOUS BORDER *is an English institution, rarely carried out in the grand manner in Australia. This one is at* Mawallok *in Victoria. Gravel is a pleasant material for wide formal paths like these, where brick or stone would be hard; but the picture is dependent on immaculate maintenance.*

Victorian extravagance

By the time Queen Victoria came to the throne, there were wealthy colonial gentlemen who could afford to build mansions and surround them with extensive gardens embellished with ornamental trees — the oaks and elms of England where it was cool enough to grow them, and the more luxuriant of the native rainforest trees — the figs, bunya pines and palms, where it was not. It was an age of exploration, and new, exotic plants and flowers were being sent to the leading English nurseries from all over the world — camellias and chrysanthemums from the Orient, dahlias from Mexico, gladioli from South Africa. Australian gardeners lost no time in importing them; status-conscious gardeners longed to upstage their neighbours with the latest fancy varieties. Anyone who could afford to, made an elaborate garden of flowers, usually planted in combinations and colour schemes that would strike us today as fussy and gaudy.

It required a lot of work too, as anyone who has tried to recreate such a garden will know, but to say that is to miss an important point. For the flower garden was the Victorian wife's domain, a place where she could spend an hour or so chatting to a friend out of husbandly earshot, under the pretext of disbudding the dahlias or admiring the amaranthus.

The twentieth century

You can still see the Victorian style surviving in many suburban parks, with their beds of multi-coloured annuals among the specimen trees. The idea that a garden was essentially a place for displays of flowers lingered on well into the twentieth century.

True, gardens looked different after the Great War. Victorian intricacy went out of fashion, speeded on its way by the increasing cost of gardeners, and wider availability of town water allowed a new emphasis on lawns, to be set off by borders of flowering shrubs 'like a picture in its frame' as one garden book of the 1930s put it. But the 'garden' remained as before at the front of the house, the backyard still being given over to the clothes line, the vegetables and the outhouse.

Changing lifestyles

It was not until after World War II that Australian gardens really began to change. More people owned a house and garden than ever before — we still have the highest per capita rate of home ownership in the world — and post-war prosperity meant more leisure. Television brought us new American ideas of 'outdoor living', a tradition familiar to the many immigrants from southern Europe. The new supermarkets relieved many people of the bother of growing their own vegetables, and modern plumbing meant that the outhouse could go: Australians were able to think of patios, barbecues and swimming pools.

Native gardens

By the 1960s a new appreciation of the beauty of our own landscape led to native plants being given their rightful place in our gardens. Though many who hoped that the 'bush garden' was the way to a beautiful garden without any work were to be disappointed, the native trees they planted have changed our suburbs for the better — for in our generally hot climate shade is no mere luxury.

In recent years, suburban gardens have become smaller as we begin to run short of land to expand our cities, and people have been returning from the suburbs to the city to live. Tiny city backyards, originally planned only for the washing and the outhouse, are being transformed into outdoor living rooms, and with the recent growth of the heritage movement, 'old-fashioned' and 'cottage' gardens are becoming more popular.

THE VICTORIAN GARDEN *in the twentieth century — flowers, shrubs, immaculate lawn — a hobby rather than a place to live.*

THIS IS NOT *an original colonial vegetable garden — the early settlers wouldn't have had the luxury of brick paving — but it is designed in the same spirit and would look appropriate next to a cottage of the period.*

The future?

What will come next? Subtropical gardens using the plants that in Europe and most of the U.S. can only be grown in greenhouses? Desert gardens, as we realise how precious water is on this driest of Earth's continents?

TYPES OF GARDENS

The garden you end up with may not be completely of your choosing. If you build on a bushland site for example, it will be cheaper, easier and, in the end, probably more pleasing, to retain the bush and design your garden around it rather than opt for a formal garden.

A shady city garden will perhaps require ferns and palms rather than a cottage garden display of annuals.

Your garden site, its aspect, its shelter, soil, size, all have to be considered in deciding on the type of garden you choose.

Even an Emperor needs a garden in which to stroll and relax his heart...
The Emperor Ch'ien Lung

"If you're in a slight daze Don't enter this maze"

THIS IS THE *garden room at the top left of the plan, with its box-edged beds overflowing with summer flowers. The paths are much narrower than would normally be comfortable — but as they don't lead anywhere but to the flowers this doesn't matter.*

A FORMAL GARDEN

There are two great problems that beset the enthusiastic gardener: first, how to accommodate the new plants and ideas that one finds one just can't forego trying; and second, how to prevent a garden that is gorgeous at its peak from collapsing into a wilderness when it is not.

This garden triumphantly solves both. Though not at all large, it is divided into a series of garden rooms, any one of which could be completely replanted without upsetting the others (and the plantings in the individual beds are regularly changed). Its formal, geometric layout holds it all together and is pleasing to look at in the off-seasons and even when that new, super-duper plant fails to perform — something that happens more often than any gardener will admit.

The rich variety of plants is the icing on the cake; this garden would look good even if many of its beds were planted with the simplest of ground-covers. Here lies another reason that the formal garden is enjoying a revival after a couple of hundred years in eclipse: its beauty resides chiefly in its architectural lines and proportions and it can be surprisingly labour-saving. Plant it with suitable, easy-care plants, and it will not be dependent on elaborate gardening for success.

ABOVE LEFT: *The brick terrace is large enough for dining; small deciduous trees on the north side give summer shade, which doesn't reach to the formal herb and flower garden at a slightly higher level. From here it presents a mass of greenery and flowers against the backdrop of the lattice walls of the toolshed and garage.*

ABOVE RIGHT: *The grass walk and its fruit trees. This one is netted to protect the fruit from birds. Notice how the use of brick paving — here edging the beds and lawn — ties the whole garden together.*

THE PLAN *of the garden, with (clockwise from mid-left): the brick terrace shown on this page, the box-edged formal flower garden on the opposite page, the simple vegetable garden, and the grass walk (above). Dividing a garden into a series of 'rooms' like this allows full use of the available space, making the whole seem much larger than it really is.*

INFORMAL, FLOWERY GARDENS

It's not uncommon, particularly in old suburbs, to find the house set so far back from the street that the front garden is considerably larger than the back. It can be tempting to increase its privacy with a tall fence, assuming the local council will allow it; but if the street is a quiet one, might this not be overreacting? And when the house is as handsome as this turn of the century stone villa in Adelaide, wouldn't it be a pity to hide it?

The plan of this garden is simple but effective. The driveway runs up the side of the house, the garage being at the back. Next to it a brick path leads to the front door. Lightly-foliaged trees along the boundaries provide a screen from the street as well as afternoon shade without masking the house unduly. In the beds beneath them grow an assortment of cottage-garden flowers, chosen with an eye to their foliage as well as their seasonal bloom. A pretty birdbath makes a centrepiece to the lawn in the Edwardian style, and the oval bed around it showcases sun-loving annuals.

The owners can sit on the front verandah and enjoy the view of the garden, without being disturbed by passers-by, who can enjoy glimpses of the house and garden.

THE TWO URNS *in the distance mark the point where visitors can leave the path to cross the lawn. Specimen plants (clipped box, say) would do the job too — but the urns add an appropriate old-fashioned touch.*

IN ANOTHER ADELAIDE GARDEN *a cottage-style planting in shades of red and pink, against a green backdrop.*

THE PLAN *of the garden shown above left. A path from the front door to the street would have destroyed the feeling of enclosure.*

GARDENS ON HILLSIDES

The problem with a hillside site is that outdoor living calls for level space, and you have to adjust the shape of the land a bit — or a lot — to get it.

How easily this can be done depends largely on how skilfully the architect and builder have fitted the house to the land; but in any event you're likely to end up with a multi-level garden. No great harm in that; after all, people have been known to contrive level changes on flat sites just for the interest they bring. But do draw *sections* of your garden as you do your doodle plans — it's easy to forget that the land isn't as flat as the paper and end up with the barbecue in the middle of a steep bank.

TOP: *The flaming chalices of the oriental poppy, a lover of dry-summer climates.*

TERRACING IS THE TRADITIONAL — *and expensive* — *way of dealing with a hillside. These owners were fortunate to find the old dry-stone walls in place* — *they date from the time the cottage in the Adelaide hills was built. With a canopy of trees and clumpy, cottagy plants, the result is the charm that only an overgrown old garden can give. Easy stairs link the various levels, which offer a seemingly endless choice of places to sit and listen to the birds.*

It's an easy-care garden — *it has to be. Who could face carting a wheelbarrow of compost up and down all those steps?*

Landscaping your garden

THIS BRISBANE HOUSE *shows what can be achieved when house and garden are considered together. By shaping the house almost as a series of pavilions stepping up the hill, the architect has been able to create courtyard gardens at each level. From street level the only hint of their presence is foliage rising between the roofs. Completely private and self-contained they are linked by paths at the side of the house so there is no need to trundle the wheelbarrow through the rooms.*

THINK OF PLANNING a hillside garden like a split-level house with rooms on different levels, each planned for different activities — but remember to make access from one level to another easy and comfortable, bearing in mind that sometimes you'll be carrying heavy objects like pot plants or furniture.

RIGHT: *A grassy two-level garden opens straight off the living room at its upper level, off the kitchen at the lower. Lower still is an entry court, higher up again the bedrooms look out onto trees and greenery of their own.*

BELOW: *A protea, flourishing in the upper courtyard where it is sheltered from hot winds.*

BUSHLAND GARDENS

If you build on a bushland site, you have the opportunity to create the sort of garden that romantic gardeners have dreamed of ever since gardens have been made — untouched nature. It isn't really untouched of course, the very act of building is a drastic intervention in the ecology of your surroundings, but with care you can go a long way to heal the scars and create the illusion that all is what it was before.

Start, if you can, before you build by instructing your builder to confine his operations to as small an area of the site as possible, and to take his rubbish away — you don't want to be trying to camouflage piles of spoil from excavations or heaps of broken bricks (it's bad enough in any garden).

Keep the trees
Preserve, at the very least, as many trees as you can, even ones that aren't especially beautiful in themselves — the bush isn't made up of perfect specimens. They are the bones of your landscape; they create the mulch of fallen leaves and give shelter to the wildlife that will return when the builder goes.

Lawns, neat beds, anything that smacks of cultivation, are out. Patios and living areas are perhaps best kept closely associated with the house, extending its character in contrast with the 'untouched' areas where you might have paths of fallen leaves, casually maintained gravel, stone or heavy timber steps... it all depends on the feeling of the site, on what 'it wants to be' as the Japanese say.

You may want to dress nature up a little, maybe clearing undergrowth that's obscuring a handsome rock, maybe extending a colony of ferns, adding more trees to complete a group; but if ever the old saw about art concealing art was true, it's in the making of a garden like this.

You'll need to add plants — shrubs maybe, and groundcovers, but don't overplant. And resist the temptation to plant a wide variety of species, even if they are native (ideally, native to your area) — nature usually plants very simply. Take your time. Much of your gardening will be the removal of weeds and interlopers which always seem to come in from nowhere, but as the garden restores itself, the need will grow less.

A POINT to take very seriously: we live in a land of bushfires, and you need to be fire-aware. Take all the usual precautions — keeping your gutters clear and so on — and consider providing emergency water tanks and water outlets in the garden. Many a house has been saved by the sprinklers being turned on in times of peril. Your local fire brigade knows the conditions, and will be happy to give you advice.

NOT SO LONG AGO, *this rainforest gully was overgrown with an impenetrable thicket of privet and lantana. With their removal — a big job — and the planting of palms and ferns, it looks something like its former self. Observe the restraint with which the new plants have been used; any more would just have created another overgrown tangle.*

Landscaping your garden

ABOVE: *Not really a bushland garden — but the trees that were retained when this Darwin house was built saved it from the force of Cyclone Tracy.*

RIGHT: *Here the bones of the garden are the magnificent rock outcrops and the gnarled old banksias. Might the steps in the background have looked better if they had been cut into the rock and washed down with liquid manure to age them?*

FAR RIGHT: *Every tree that could be saved was, and with the restoration of the groundcover of ferns and small shrubs, and the gradual accumulation of leaf litter, it looks as though the virgin bush has returned.*

CITY GARDENS

In a townhouse garden as small as this one — it's only six metres by ten — the temptation is to pave the lot to get maximum space. But here, by bringing planting out from the boundary walls, two garden rooms have been created, a forecourt linking the gate and the front door and a sitting room beyond.

Ivy pushes the walls into the background, and planting within the garden has been kept low and airy to avoid an overstuffed effect. Silver birches assist the large tree that was already there in screening the view of the neighbours' second storey windows. Beneath them a wide variety of shade-loving greenery flourishes, supplemented with just a few flowers — the tulips shown here will be followed by impatiens and coleus for summer colour.

The severe steel gate is a nice touch, giving the owners a look at what is happening in the world outside and passers-by a tantalising glimpse of the garden just inside. The basket-weave pattern in the brick paving is one of the easiest to lay and to design with — you can add or subtract squares without having to cut the bricks. Flowing right through the garden, it ties the whole thing together.

LOOKING FROM THE HOUSE *to the gate (top) and across into the 'sitting room' (left). You see the same large dark trunked tree (an elm) and its attendant silver birch in both pictures; the garden is very much smaller than the camera makes it appear.*

Landscaping your garden

BELOW: *The garden set for visitors, with the car banished to the street. You can just see the roller shutter on the left.*

BELOW RIGHT: Dichondra repens *is a native ground-hugger that is often recommended as a substitute for grass, as it can be walked on, grows in sun or shade, and doesn't have to be mowed. It does, however, need plenty of water and, not being really weed-proof, has to be hand-weeded, a tedious job on a full scale lawn but no great worry for a pocket handkerchief sized one like this.*

The car and the backyard

It is always desirable to be able to park the car off the street — but what do you do when the car would take up half an already tiny, oddly-shaped backyard?

Here is a brilliant compromise. The car is let in through a roller-door painted to match the walls and is banished to the street on weekends and when there are visitors. Its standing space then becomes a patio for people. A raised bed, squaring off the awkward angle of the plot, allows for some shrubs and flowers, but most of the greenery is provided by cladding the high walls all around with Virginia creeper (*Parthenocissus*) which needs no trellis to climb and takes up next to no floor space. It could be augmented with flowering vines like jasmine, moonflowers, or even climbing roses if you wished. The dense foliage not only looks good, it cuts down the reflected heat from the masonry that used to turn the garden into an oven every summer. The eye is drawn down into the garden by the panel of *Dichondra* lawn, in the centre of which a tiny pond contains a single water lily.

With potplants moved into place, you'd hardly know the car had ever been there, except for the occasional spot of oil which, the paving being treated with a proprietary masonry sealer, is easily wiped up.

Privacy

On a country property, the question of privacy may hardly arise, the neighbours are far away. In a large suburban garden, there's room for banks of shrubs, even if the fences are only the usual 1.5 metres high. But in a very small place, the problem of ensuring that you won't feel you're conducting your life under the public gaze can determine much of your garden planning. It usually isn't so much the presence of the neighbours themselves in *their* gardens (unless you happen to dislike them), but their windows — most of us find the idea of being watched by unseen eyes distinctly unnerving.

Types of gardens

A long narrow backyard

When the garden is long and narrow, as this one is, and overlooked by high buildings to boot, the problem becomes acute. High walls would create a cooped-up feeling, and there just isn't room for tall shrubs to spread themselves. Trees, quite substantial ones, proved the answer. They take up little usable space, as you can walk under them, and even the winter-bare branches of deciduous trees like these give a sense of protection.

Simplicity gives a sense of space

The plan is straightforward — virtually wall-to-wall brick paving, wide enough so that it doesn't look like a path to nowhere, with the trees and lower plantings hard against the fences on either side. There's subtlety too, in the way the corridor-like perspective is broken — first by changing the pattern of the bricks at either end, and then by the two semi-circular beds that jut into the space at the far end so that you have to walk around them to the side gate.

LOOKING DOWN *the length of the garden from the house. Beds seen at an acute angle like this always seem lusher than they do seen straight on. The big tree behind the table and chairs is a golden elm (Ulmus 'Marie van Houtte' or vanhouttiana).*

THE VIEW BACK *to the house from the gate. Permanent furniture would clutter a small space like this, so the owners bring out directors' chairs and a folding table as they need them.*

ABOVE AND LEFT: *The planting in the beds, apart from the odd bulky grower like the strelitzia, is kept low-growing to avoid crowding the narrow space too much; creepers clothe the fences, and the occasional low plant is allowed to spill onto the pavement and break its lines.*

Low Maintenance Gardens

ALL INFANT GARDENS need constant attention — it's only as they begin to establish themselves that even the most carefully thought-out 'low-maintenance' gardens earn the title.

'Give me a beautiful garden that never needs any work!' is a universal cry but in fact the work-free garden is as impossible a dream as the house which never needs cleaning.

You *could* pave the place entirely (green concrete?) and 'plant' it with artificial plants — but wouldn't it be a soulless kind of place? And you'd still have to sweep the concrete and dust the 'plants' as the Los Angeles freeway people found a few years ago when they tried 'landscaping' with plastic palm trees growing out of carpets of plastic daisies; it proved cheaper to look after real plants after all.

The essence of a garden is that it is *alive*; its quiet rhythms of growth, burgeoning and decay are those of nature itself. That is why people whose task it is to mend broken souls so often prescribe gardening for therapy. But for all that, none of us wants to be a slave to our garden. It makes sense to take care not to design any more work into it than we have to.

How much work is too much?

To a great extent, the answer depends on your expectations of what a garden should be. If your heart is set on lavish and constant displays of flowers, or if you shudder at the thought of a leaf out of place, you'll be spending more time gardening than someone who is content with a mainly green garden, adorned with such flowers as and when easy-care plants choose to produce them.

Garden work comes under two headings: the care that plants need to grow well, and what we might call garden housework — raking leaves, weeding, mowing the lawn — and with forethought you can reduce both of these to a minimum.

MOWING THE LAWN *is the least loved of garden chores. But if you naturalise bulbs in the grass as the English do (right), you'll get a show of flowers in spring and relief from mowing from the time the bulbs come up until they die down — if you can put up with their after-flowering tattiness. These are daffodils, but freesias, sparaxis and their kind will be just as pretty in a warm climate. Or (opposite) you could create a flowering meadow, an idea popular in America. Who could bear to cut down these daisies? Californian poppies, coreopsis or gazanias would be good too — but don't try to make a meadow where the grass is too lush.*

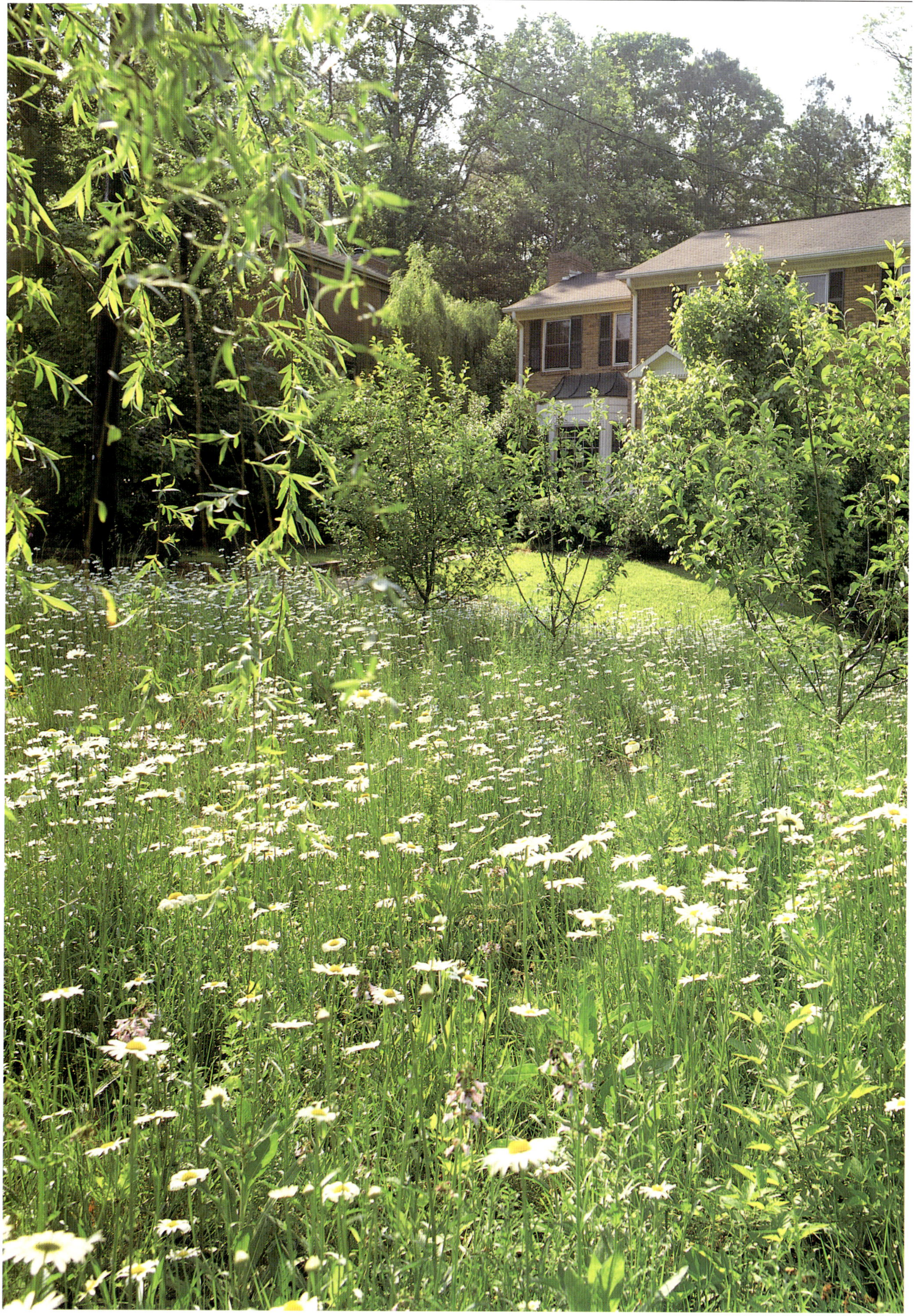

A MASSED PLANTING of gazanias and arctotis, needing a little in the way of care for a long season of beauty.

Awake thou wind and blow upon my garden, that the spices thereof may flow out...
The Song of Solomon

Easy-care plants

What is an easy-care plant, the kind any sensible gardener makes the backbone of his plantings? Ideally, it should flourish and delight you with no attention other than admiration, or at least with no more than you think it is worth. If it flourishes mightily but bores you stiff, then don't grow it; but on the other hand, don't fall into the common gardener's mistake of equating rarity and difficulty with beauty. And remember that a plant that grows with no care in another part of the country may be an invalid in yours, if your climate and soil are not to its liking.

Before you decide to grow any plant, ask yourself: Will it grow well *here*, in my climate and soil? Does it need regular watering? Fertiliser? Spraying against pests and diseases? Does it have to be pruned to look presentable or to flower or fruit well? (Roses and most fruit trees do, but many plants that are usually pruned regularly can get by quite well without — crepe myrtles for instance.) Is it likely to outgrow its allotted position, so that it will need constant cutting back? (Watch this one carefully — misjudging the final size of plants is one of the commonest sources of unwanted work. Many plants *can* be kept much smaller than they would grow naturally, bougainvillea for instance, but the minute you turn your back they'll be off and away again.) Is it invasive, needing to be kept from taking over? (Bamboo is the classic example.) Does it make a mess, shedding leaves, bark or fruit where they'll be a nuisance? The importance you place on this depends to an extent on where you plan to plant — a rain of gum leaves can be allowed to fall among shrubs where they'll make a mulch; you probably won't be so happy with having to sweep them off the patio and you certainly won't be delighted with having to scoop them out of the swimming pool.

If you can answer yes to the first question and no to all the others, then you have an easy-care plant, and you'll find there are plenty of them to choose from, wherever your garden might be.

Garden housework

Of the housework jobs, weeding should not become a burden if you get rid of the perennial nasties before you plant; then mulching and dense planting should keep further invasions at bay. But there will always be some — console yourself with the thought that if your soil couldn't grow weeds then it wouldn't grow anything else either.

Do you need a lawn?

Lawnmowing, and its attendant trimming of the edges, is most people's pet hate. Why not consider eliminating lawn altogether? You could pave and gravel the places where you want to walk, as they often do in Italy, or you could lay the garden out as a woodland with much of it floored in leaves or tanbark, making extensive use of groundcovers in the American manner. Such gardens are for grown-ups; if children are to play and tumble, there's still no better surface than grass.

It's easy to get obsessive about the perfect lawn, but does it really matter if it's sometimes a bit shaggy or if clover gets in, even a few dandelions? Keep it a simple shape — no difficult-to-get-at odd corners or wriggly curves — and don't clutter it with little beds to trim around. Don't put grass where it's too steep to mow comfortably; banks are best planted with shrubs or groundcovers.

Watch the junction of grass and groundcovers carefully; they'll invariably try to invade one another and you'll be constantly on your knees trying to keep them apart. Where you want grass sweeping up to your plantings, make the plants knee-high shrubs, set densely. Then you can tuck the mower under their outside branches, and mow under their overhang — and you won't have a visible edge to trim.

Above all, don't make the beginner's mistake of planting a fast-growing grass like perennial rye or the wildly invasive kikuyu. Sure, the finer, slow growing grasses are more trouble to establish, but you have to mow them only half as often.

A Victorian Style Garden

THIS ISN'T ACTUALLY A VICTORIAN HOUSE, but the garden with its masses of flowers in large beds separated by generous gravel paths is very much in the mid-nineteenth century tradition.

The owner has brought the style up to date, concentrating on long-blooming perennials suited to her dry-summer climate and planting them in an informal arrangement of roughly oval beds, rather than in the usual Victorian symmetrical layout of circles, squares and crescents.

Dense plantings of tall shrubs, mostly natives, provide privacy along the boundaries. Even the backyard is mostly gravel and shrubs; the total elimination of lawn allows the gardener to spend her time looking after her flowers, which she enjoys, instead of mowing, weeding, and watering grass, which she doesn't. Only a keen gardener should attempt a garden such as this — a few months' neglect would reduce it to tatters. When properly cared for, it looks charming with the house afloat on its sea of flowers.

A LOW-MAINTENANCE CITY GARDEN

ABOVE: *Bluebells* (Endymion hispanicus)

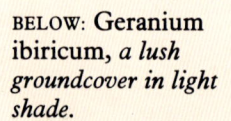

BELOW: Geranium ibiricum, *a lush groundcover in light shade.*

This wonderfully casual garden is about as close to the work-free garden as it's possible to get. Only five minutes from the city, it isn't large, but it could be three times the size without being any more demanding.

Originally there was a walnut tree, which the owner liked and kept, and a leaky above-ground pool and some lawn, both of which were removed. Now there is a patio, paved in concrete bricks and shaded with a pergola covered in banana passionfruit; a jungle of mainly native shrubs and small trees around the outside for privacy; and, growing in a thick mulch, an assortment of groundcovers and clumpy things, with some daffodils and bluebells for a splash of colour in spring. 'I just plant anything I like the look of,' says the owner, 'and if it likes me I plant more.' The reward for such boldness is that all the gardening — apart from planting — is spreading some fertiliser when it rains and pulling out the odd weed that dares to show its head.

RIGHT: *Low maintenance doesn't mean none at all — a neglected garden doesn't give a display of flowers like this. But this isn't a laborious garden — much of the plantings are of easy-care shrubs and perennials, and grass has been almost eliminated in favour of paving.*

Types of gardens

NATIVE GARDENS

Gardening with the native plants of one's country has a long tradition; the ancient Greeks did it, so did the Japanese, and the famous old gardens of France and Italy feature the same trees that are seen in the surrounding countryside.

The dinky-di garden
Alas, the decision to follow suit in Australia is often prompted by a kind of horticultural ockerism — 'no foreign rubbish in *my* garden, mate!' — rather than a real appreciation of the unique and subtle beauty of our native plants. The result is all too often a hodgepodge, with plants from Western Australia cheek by jowl with others from the Queensland rainforests and such things as the hybrid Grevilleas, which are (for all their beauty) native only to gardens and nurseries.

There's no need to go to the extreme of only growing plants native to your area, though it makes sense to use them (and their garden varieties) as the basis of your planting. As with any other plants in the garden, the question is, do they look happy together? You'll find it easier to harmonise a fairly limited selection rather than a collection of one of this and one of that.

FAR LEFT: *A native garden might not achieve the massed colour that one planted with exotics can — most Australian plants are too modest for that — but it can still be thrilling in its way. Here an acacia lights up a mainly green garden like a burst of spring sunshine.*

LEFT: *The callistemons or bottlebrushes are great shrubs for a place where they won't dry out. As well as the familiar scarlet, they come in a range of colours from white to pink and mauve, and in habit from small shrubs to trees.*

ABOVE: Eucalyptus caesia. *The beauty of native flowers is often only revealed on close inspection.*

LEFT: *The hybrid banksia 'Giant Candles' is as spectacular as any exotic shrub. Here it is perfectly contrasted with the brighter but smaller flowers of* Grevillea lavandulacea.

THIS GARDEN *(and its house) in Victoria were designed by the late Alistair Knox, one of the pioneers of native garden design. At first sight, it looks as though the house has just been set down in a pretty patch of bushland, but a lot of clearing was done to build the house and what you see in the pictures is in fact a garden.*

Both local plants and others from elsewhere in Australia have been blended with great skill; nothing stands out as obviously contrived, yet the result is a garden. Lusher and more flowery than the nearby bushland, it offers quiet and tranquil places for family living.

Don't forget people

Of course, the native garden is as much a place for people as any other — don't allow your enthusiasm for the plants make you forget to create places for sitting, for the children to play, and for all the other non-gardening things you want to do. While the native flora provides plants for most purposes — screening shrubs, groundcovers, fence-hiding climbers and so on — in one respect it lets you down. There are no deciduous trees for summer shade and winter sun except for the Tasmanian *Nothofagus gunnii* and that is only a large shrub in cultivation. This means that you either have to design without deciduous trees, or (horrors!) introduce foreign ones. Still, native and exotic plants can be blended with success — Californian gardeners grow many Australian (and New Zealand) plants alongside their own natives and plants from other parts of the world.

The 'natural look' native garden

It is possible to use native plants in a formal design, but they lend themselves best to a more casual style of garden. Gravel or a softly coloured paving is often better as a background than the sharp green of lawn grass. They require less maintenance too, but the notion that a native garden needs no work is a fantasy; native plants benefit from care as much as any others do.

WHILE IT'S TRUE that they often need less water and fertiliser than most foreigners, and many are gratifyingly fast-growing, native plants are frequently distressingly short-lived, and to keep a native garden looking in its prime after ten years or so calls for regular replanting. No great worry if you are aware it's going to happen (and plan accordingly) but upsetting if you aren't.

RIGHT: *Banksia ericifolia, one of the most reliable of a much-admired but often temperamental genus.*

FAR RIGHT: *Pittosporum rhombifolium from Queensland, one of the most spectacular of all berry-bearing shrubs.*

= Types of gardens =

The Collector's Garden

ROSES: *'Elizabeth of Glamis' (left) and 'Red Planet' (above).*

BELOW LEFT: *In the foreground, a spray of white blossoms of a flowering plum, whose red–brown leaves will echo the young leaves of the roses. A clump of kangaroo paws gives spiky leaves to contrast with the soft grey of* Grevillea glabrata, *with white 'Iceberg' roses to follow.*

BELOW: *Looking from the house down the length of the garden, the pear trees are about to bloom, and on either side of the lawn are fragrant herbs — rosemary, mint and peppermint geraniums. The main rosebed stretches almost all the way across the garden in the middle distance.*

THERE IS A BREED OF GARDENER for whom the greatest joy of gardening is the bringing to perfection of a particular, beloved flower. What happens if the beloved takes over the garden as an ever-expanding collection demands more and more planting space? If it makes for happiness, why not? But it is possible to cater for a special flower without unbalancing the garden. The secret is, paradoxically enough, to plan the basic framework without it, so that the garden will still look good in the off-seasons.

A ROSE GARDEN. Here is an example, a small Adelaide garden belonging to a rose-lover who started out by deciding that the garden wouldn't be just a 'rose factory'. (The pictures were taken in early spring, without a rose to be seen, so you can judge how successful it is.) The long block is divided into three parts: near the house a lawn, framed by two flowering pears (still young); in the middle, the main rose beds, divided by a path running diagonally towards the back gate; beyond, a space for shade-loving flowers beneath a big lemon tree, the only worthwhile plant in the original garden.

Right at the top of the block, a small plot next to the garage was intended for vegetables — but they didn't last long — it proved too tempting to use the space for more roses.

61

Seaside Gardens

Garden-making by the sea poses its own special problems. To begin with, you have to strike a balance between openness to the ocean view and providing shelter from the sea wind, which isn't always a gentle zephyr — with its teeth sharpened by salt picked up from the sea spray the wind can cut any plant that gets in its way as effectively as a pair of pruning shears. It takes a dense mass of growth to deflect the sea wind and protect plants that are not native to the seaside. If your site is blessed with a stand of native trees — banksias, teatrees or casuarinas, think twice before clearing them away; they can make the basis of a very pleasant garden.

ABOVE: *The Gazania does so well by the seaside that it has become almost a cliché.*

RIGHT: *The Gymea or giant lily grows very well in sandy soil but the 4 metre tall flower stems need protection from the wind.*

IN THE SHELTER *of a natural (but tidied up) teatree scrub, ferns and groundcovers make a lush fringe for a brick path.*

Types of gardens

THE HOUSE *itself affords some shelter, and even if you keep the seaward side of the garden open and low, trees to landward will help give shelter for salt-hating plants.*

ABOVE: *In a sunny spot, a mixed planting of arctotis and alyssum, both happy in sandy soil.*

LEFT: *With their lower dead branches removed, the teatrees reveal attractive lines. Every so often, an old one falls over and groundcovers and shrubs are allowed to grow over and around it.*

RAILWAY SLEEPER STEPS, *set in a carpet of mulch and groundcovers, carry out the informal theme of this garden.*

The soil

This is liable to be poor stuff, sandy and thirsty — hungry for compost too; if your place is a weekender, you'll be wanting to hold maintenance to a minimum so that you can spend your time sailing, sunning or swimming.

A bushland seaside garden

The owners of the garden on these pages, which overlooks Port Phillip Bay, decided not to clear away the teatree (*Leptospermum*) scrub, contenting themselves with some discreet pruning and thinning, making the garden in the resulting sheltered glades. Though the wide view of the sea from the garden is sacrificed, there are still glimpses through the foliage.

The tea-trees set the informal bushland theme; there is no lawn, and except for the main paths linking the house with the gate, the barbecue or the fenced work area where the compost heaps are (which are mostly brick), you walk on a carpet of pine bark and tea-tree leaves. There are lots of groundcovers and sufficient shelter to grow tender plants like azaleas and fuchsias. These need constant watering in the sandy soil, no great hardship in a full-time residence such as this, but a matter to watch carefully in selecting plants for a weekender.

Landscaping your garden

A SMALL VEGETABLE GARDEN, *linked to the patio by matching paving and its radiating lines, but marked off from it by a border of flowers. The pattern of beds could be extended across the lawn without spoiling the balance of the garden, and even when the beds are almost empty it still looks interesting.*

ADJACENT TO THE PATIO, *a pattern of small rectangular beds backed by a picket fence gives a pleasantly cottagey feeling, and is filled with a variety of herbs. Many herbs can be a bit nondescript in their off-seasons; an ornament like the birdbath here can make a welcome focal point.*

Kitchen Gardens

A cabbage may not be as universally admired as a rose, but a well tended kitchen garden has a beauty of its own. It's partly the beauty of good craftsmanship, partly the anticipation of culinary delights.

If you enjoy growing vegetables and herbs and bringing them to the table with pride, why not give them a place of honour in your garden plan? There's no need to create a market garden in miniature, with all the plants in rigid rows (though they are easier to tend that way) with bare earth between. Instead you can cut beds from the lawn, planting them full to overflowing (rather like an old-fashioned rose garden), make a vegetable border with shrubs or a vine-covered fence to back it up, create a strong pattern of raised beds and paving to continue the architectural lines of the house and patio, and jazz up the green of the vegies with some flowers, perhaps annuals intended for cutting for the house. As long as they get their quota of sunshine (as much as possible) they will be happy.

= Types of gardens =

A COMPLETELY UTILITARIAN *backyard, devoted entirely to vegetables — even the pergola is covered with squashes. Apart from being amazingly productive, it has charm, and its owner has every right to be proud of it.*

A POND *(with a small timber deck for viewing the fish) acts as a pivot between this luxuriant vegetable garden, the crops arranged like flowers in a cottage border, and the lawn. Annuals for cutting add a touch of colour to a composition in greens.*

ANOTHER FORMAL *herb garden, the centrepiece this time being an urn filled with plants. It needn't be planted with herbs — it would look equally well as a small rose or iris garden, the backdrop of trees setting off the flowers.*

Vegetables and herbs among the flowers

And why not let edible plants take their place in the rest of the garden? A pergola could be covered with kiwi fruit (whose white-and-gold flowers are better than just pretty) or with grapes, a fence with passionfruit; most fruit trees are as beautiful in spring as their merely ornamental cousins; herbs can lend subtle tones of green as well as scent to a cottage-style planting of mixed flowers.

EDIBLE PLANTS *can take their place as ornamentals too; here are parsley and the red stemmed silver beet ('Ruby Chard') contributing to a red-and-green colour scheme with primulas and an azalea.*

65

Making a period garden

Take on the renovation of an old house, and sooner or later the question will arise — should the garden be re-created in period style to match?

ITS NAME *long forgotten, this rose was rescued from an old garden.*

THOSE WHO FEEL that a house isn't right unless everything from cornices to coffee cups is 'correct' for the time the house was built will probably say it should; but most of us will be content with a less purist approach. For one thing, 'correctness' in garden style is very difficult to pin down; gardeners have always gardened to suit themselves, without quite the concern for changing fashion that architects and interior decorators have shown; and for another, a garden matures and changes with the years. A marble fireplace will look much the same now as it did when it was made in 1880, but would you want to cut down a majestic hundred year-old tree and replace it with a sapling to 'restore' the garden to the way it looked in, say, 1895?

THIS PIONEER'S COTTAGE *in South Australia has been rebuilt from its ruins by the great-grandson of the man who built it. Purists might argue that the original garden would have been a jumble of flowers, vegetables and chicken runs. Perhaps, but the new garden of shrubs and flowers is perfectly in keeping with the unpretentious simplicity of the house, and it's appropriate in size too — it's most unlikely that a house like this would have been surrounded by acres of garden.*

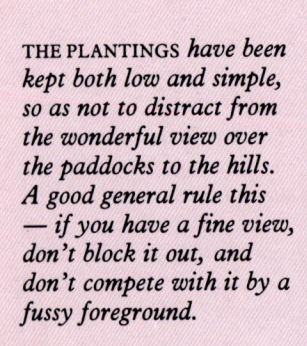

THE PLANTINGS *have been kept both low and simple, so as not to distract from the wonderful view over the paddocks to the hills. A good general rule this — if you have a fine view, don't block it out, and don't compete with it by a fussy foreground.*

Making a period garden

HERE THERE WAS NOTHING *of the original garden to guide the owner, who settled for a romantic cottage-garden mix of flowers. The white picket fence, a little taller than usual, with its matching arch over the gate is in keeping with the style of the house, as is the brick path (notice, above left, how there is a path along the length of the veranda so you can step off it at any point). The veranda is wide enough for sitting out, so most of the garden can be devoted to an assortment of favourite flowers, mostly in pale feminine shades, like the old favourite rose 'Madame Butterfly' (top).*

The problems of re-creating a period garden

A house can fall into ruins and still preserve enough evidence of what it once was to allow you to re-create its original appearance perfectly; a neglected garden may well disappear entirely — and if an old garden has been loved and looked after it may well now be very different from its original state.

This gives you a great deal of freedom; if the 'architectural' details of the garden (the fences, gates and steps) are original or replacements in the appropriate style, you can plan your plantings in any way you like to create a pleasant setting for your house and lifestyle. Isn't that what the gardeners of the old days did too?

OLD PHOTOGRAPHS can be a great aid in reconstructing a garden. If your house has been in your family for years, you may have some. Otherwise a talk to your local historical society — the council can probably put you in touch — may unearth old records. And long-time residents often have long memories.

THE IRON FENCE *may be original, but it doesn't fit the Federation style of the cottage (the left side of the pair), and the front garden is non-existent.*

67

Plants and Planting

There's no need to speak at length on the importance of plants; most of us find it difficult to imagine a garden without them. Even the rock-and-sand gardens of Japanese temples contain moss and lowly herbs, and are framed and set off by ancient trees.

Without a backbone of permanent planting — shrubs and trees, creepers on fences — the beauty of a garden is as ephemeral as a flower arrangement. When the petunias are over, what is there to look at?

Plant for a purpose

Of all the tasks facing the garden-maker, the selection of the right plants can be the most daunting. There are so *many* plants offering themselves for consideration, and they will insist on introducing themselves by jaw-breaking Latin names, no-one could possibly be familiar with them all. How to choose the right ones for your purpose?

The 'secret' is to remember the purpose, the role you need the plant to play. Covering the ground, the vegetable equivalent of paving? Something about ankle-height, with dense, weed-suppressing foliage. A wall of greenery for privacy? A dense, maybe evergreen, shrub, head-height at least, and so on. This both limits the choices, and helps the nurseryman to make suggestions (how frustrating it is to be asked for 'something pretty for the front garden').

You need to cultivate the habit of looking at the plant *as a whole*, not just as its flowers. How big is it, both in height and spread? Is it upright, bushy, spreading? Is it dense and solid looking, or open and transparent? Does it have glossy leaves that catch the light, or is the general effect of a matt finish? Is it bold and eye-catching, or would it be more suitable as a background plant? Is it generally a dark or pale colour (usually green)? Most importantly, is it attractive year-round? This doesn't necessarily mean that it is evergreen; many deciduous plants are handsome in their bare branches, though others become just a shapeless mass of sticks. And, a critical point, does it grow well in your soil and climate without too much attention? It's crazy to fill the garden with cot-cases, no matter how beautiful and rare.

Keep it simple

Look at plants this way, with a designer's eye, and it is surprising how the appropriate ones will suggest themselves, and how ideas for mixing and matching will emerge too, though it's almost always better to go with a simple planting of a few species than to try to weave an intricate tapestry of many. Sure, it needs courage to buy a dozen of one plant — what if it doesn't flourish? — than to hedge one's bet with a dozen different ones, but it's worth it.

In this respect, the knowledgeable gardener can be at a disadvantage in not being able to forego having all of his favourites — we all have seen horticultural zoos, full of one of this and two of that.

Make not [your garden] too busy or full of work
Francis Bacon

OPPOSITE: *Knee-high plants — lavender, coreopsis, catmint and others.*

BELOW: *If you think of the heights of plants, not in terms of metres, but in relation to people, it is much easier to imagine how they will fit into your design.*

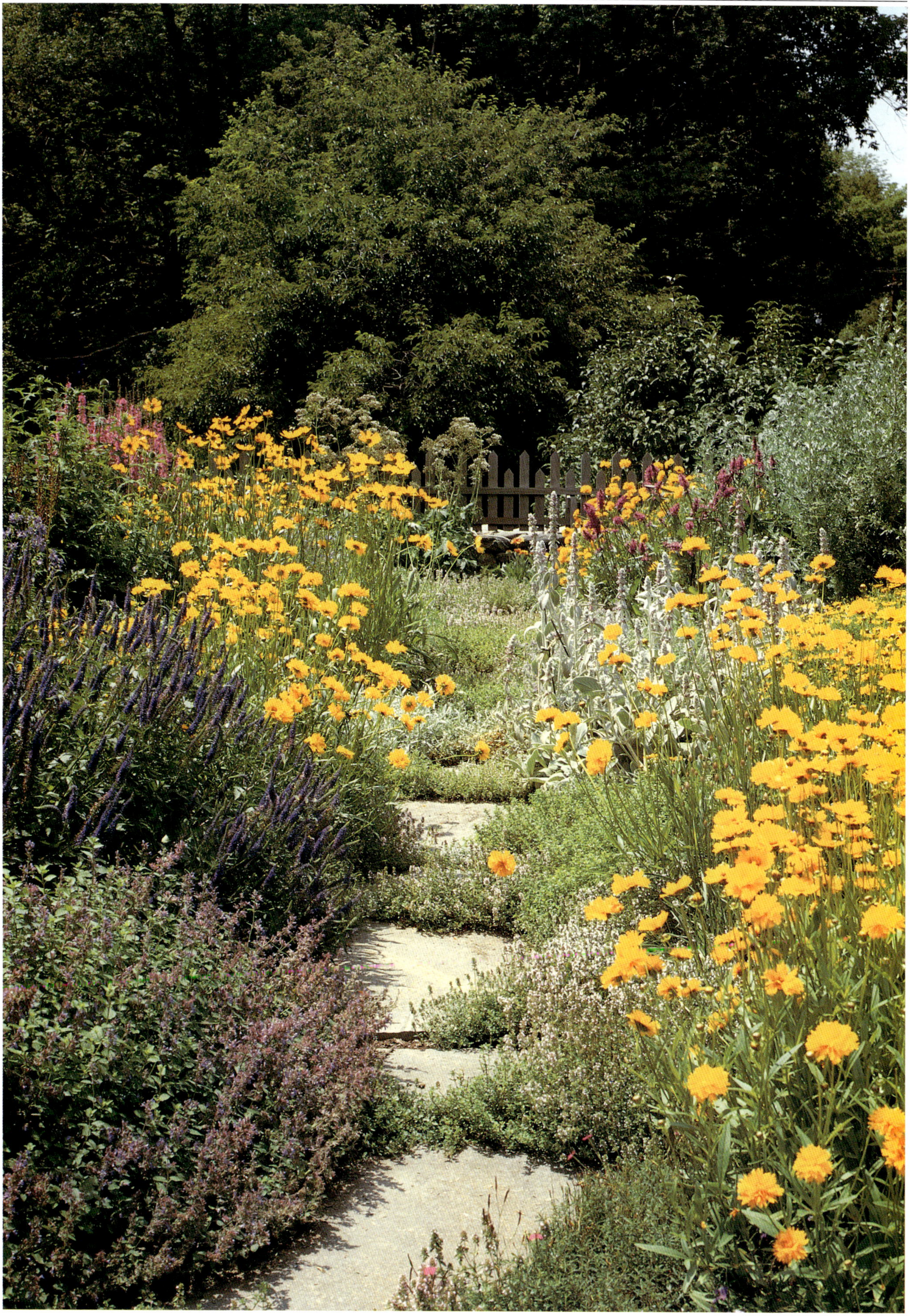

Landscaping your garden

ABOVE: *Bauhinia galpinii, not more than chest high but much wider.*

BELOW: *Where there's room for them, large shrubs holding their flowers overhead can give a wonderful romantic feeling of being drowned in flowers. Here the generously wide path is in perfect proportion to the masses of Kolkwitzias on either side. You could repeat this sort of planting on either side of a driveway too.*

LARGE SHRUBS

To the botanist, a woody plant is a shrub if it makes several main stems from ground level, and a tree if it has only one (its trunk) — the distinction is quite clear. Not so to the gardener, for whom a tree is a plant you can walk under, a shrub being a smaller affair, not a lot over head height at most, with low branches. The very largest shrubs, among them the crepe myrtles, privet, and the largest hibiscus, blur the distinction; you can either allow them to grow freely, to make great domes of growth, or turn them into small trees by judicious removal of their lower branches. This needs to be done with care if they are not to look mutilated and artificial, but it can be a handy way of retrieving the situation where someone has planted one of these very tall shrubs without allowing for its spread.

Room to grow

This is one of the commonest mistakes in garden-making; for useful as head-high shrubs are for making screens and windbreaks, they need room to spread their skirts, and if you can't give it to them, you're in for constant cutting back at best and butchered shrubs at worst.

Reference books and the descriptive labels most nurseries use have an irritating habit of not telling you the spread of shrubs, but as a general rule they will grow as wide as tall. This can be awkward in tight situations like the narrow strip one so often finds between the driveway and the side fence. Small trees are better here (or shrubs trained as trees) so that you can pass beneath, with creepers on the fence and small shrubs at their feet.

Scale

It's tempting to sloganise — something like *large shrubs are only for large gardens* — but that would be misleading. After all, you wouldn't use miniature furniture simply because your living room was small. A shrub (or a group of them) can conceal what lies on the other side more gracefully than a fence or wall — and what a feeling of luxury to pass close by flowers held out at shoulder height.

MELALEUCA LINARIIFOLIA *is a small tree — here is the 'dwarf' form, still a head-high shrub. You could use it in a hedge or an informal planting to divide the garden or for privacy.*

70

= Plants and planting =

A HEDGE *doesn't have to be either green or formal — these azaleas, lightly clipped after flowering, should be colourful enough for anyone.*

*All theory, dear friend is grey —
But the golden tree of Life springs ever green*
Goethe

HEDGES

Hedges are rather out of fashion at the moment. Perhaps it's simply that clipping is a lot of work, perhaps it's that we think of them as being a bit pretentious — the upstart gardener trying to improve on nature — perhaps we just don't see any point in them any more. After all, a row of shrubs can give just as effective a barrier as a clipped hedge can, and flowers into the bargain.

But there are situations where the strong, architectural line of a clipped hedge is appropriate. Like a wall, a formal hedge needs to look as though it is there for a definite purpose — extending the lines of a building into the landscape, or providing a solid enclosure. Give it a beginning and an end — maybe linking it to the house, leading it from a solid fence or boundary wall to a gate, or allowing it to disappear into a dense mass of shrubs.

Use your imagination when choosing plants

A hedge need not be made of greedy and boring privet; any shrub that will take the shears will do. Some of the finer-leaved grevilleas can make a dense wall of green, and the Japanese make splendid tall hedges of camellias; low ones could be made as well with scented diosma or rosemary as with the traditional box.

THE ULTIMATE *in hedging is topiary, the clipping of dense evergreens into frankly artificial shapes. (These are in England.) You either love the idea or hate it, and it is a lot of work — but a* Grevillea *peacock on the patio would be quite a conversation piece.*

LEFT: Camellia sasanqua, *an ideal hedging plant, clipped or not.*

Landscaping your garden

ABOVE: *Here grapes are trained on wires strung between the house and garage to make a shady roof for the summer — a technique much used in Spain.*

RIGHT: *The traditional clipped hedge, appropriately used on the street front of a federation house. This one is of the Japanese box (*Buxus japonica*), slower-growing and easier to maintain than the privet that would have probably been used originally. Ivy covers the arch.*

RIGHT: *The red brick wall not only looked overpowering, it reflected the heat of the afternoon sun. The solution was to slipcover it in virginia creeper, which makes a backdrop for the ornate bench, painted a startling mauve.*

FAR RIGHT: *The delicacy of* **Jasminum polyanthum** *is just right for the tea-tree fence.*

CLIMBERS

Climbing plants can be classified in two ways. First by the way they climb: a few will cling to a wall without a trellis (ivy, Virginia creeper, the climbing fig); most twine or have tendrils, so need branches or a trellis to grasp hold of (grapes, wisteria, passionfruit, the various jasmines); and some bougainvilleas, climbing roses and their ilk, send out long branches in the hope the gardener will tie them to something. Second, by the density of their growth. Some will completely smother and mask their support, so that a brick wall, for instance, is transformed into a wall of leaves. Among these are ivy, the several bignonias (which make a sheet of flowers in season), or wisteria (in leaf). Others are more restrained, and decorate their support without hiding it — wisteria (in flower), climbing roses, or the native appleberry (*Billardiera scandens*).

Your choice depends on your purpose: whether you want to completely slip-cover an unsightly construction, or draw attention to an attractive one.

> CLIMBERS HAVE a tendency to rush upwards, leaving the bottom of the wall or fence bare; forcing them to grow out horizontally at first will help to counteract the habit.

Plants and planting

IT IS THE ESSENCE *of the cottage garden style that it makes lavish use of ephemeral and flimsy plants. But the structure of this garden is still strong. The change of level with its steps (plain, weathered concrete, nothing fancy) divides the sitting area next to the house from the rest of the garden, and the arch both reinforces the division and links the two. Tall shrubs frame all and give privacy. You could replace the flowers with low-maintenance shrubs and groundcovers; without altering the plan at all, you'd have a quite different garden.*

ANNUALS AND SMALL SHRUBS

If trees and large shrubs, along with buildings, fences and pergolas (and the plants with which they may be clothed) form the structure of the garden room, annuals and herbaceous plants are its furnishings. With them we might group some of the smaller shrubs and shrubby plants like the (usually) knee-high Kurume azaleas, geraniums, or the bushy marguerites; roses too, which though they are shrubs are mostly flimsy ones.

With the structure firmly in place, you can decorate with these less substantial plants as much or as little as you please, showcasing them against the flattering backdrop of the permanent greenery; planting them in small groups in key positions, or in great sweeps; experimenting with new varieties, with changing combinations of form and colour, which is one of the joys of gardening.

Don't forget the value of their foliage — the laciness of ferns, the grassy leaves of daylilies or irises in contrast with the rounded forms of shrubs; and the eye-catching boldness of acanthus or ginger lilies.

A SINGLE SPECIES *can be used to underscore the lines of a garden room where a mixture may compete with them. Here daylilies do the job with grace; a solid painting of shrubs might have given too emphatic a line. The daylily foliage is almost evergreen, and they flower for months, from early November until autumn.*

73

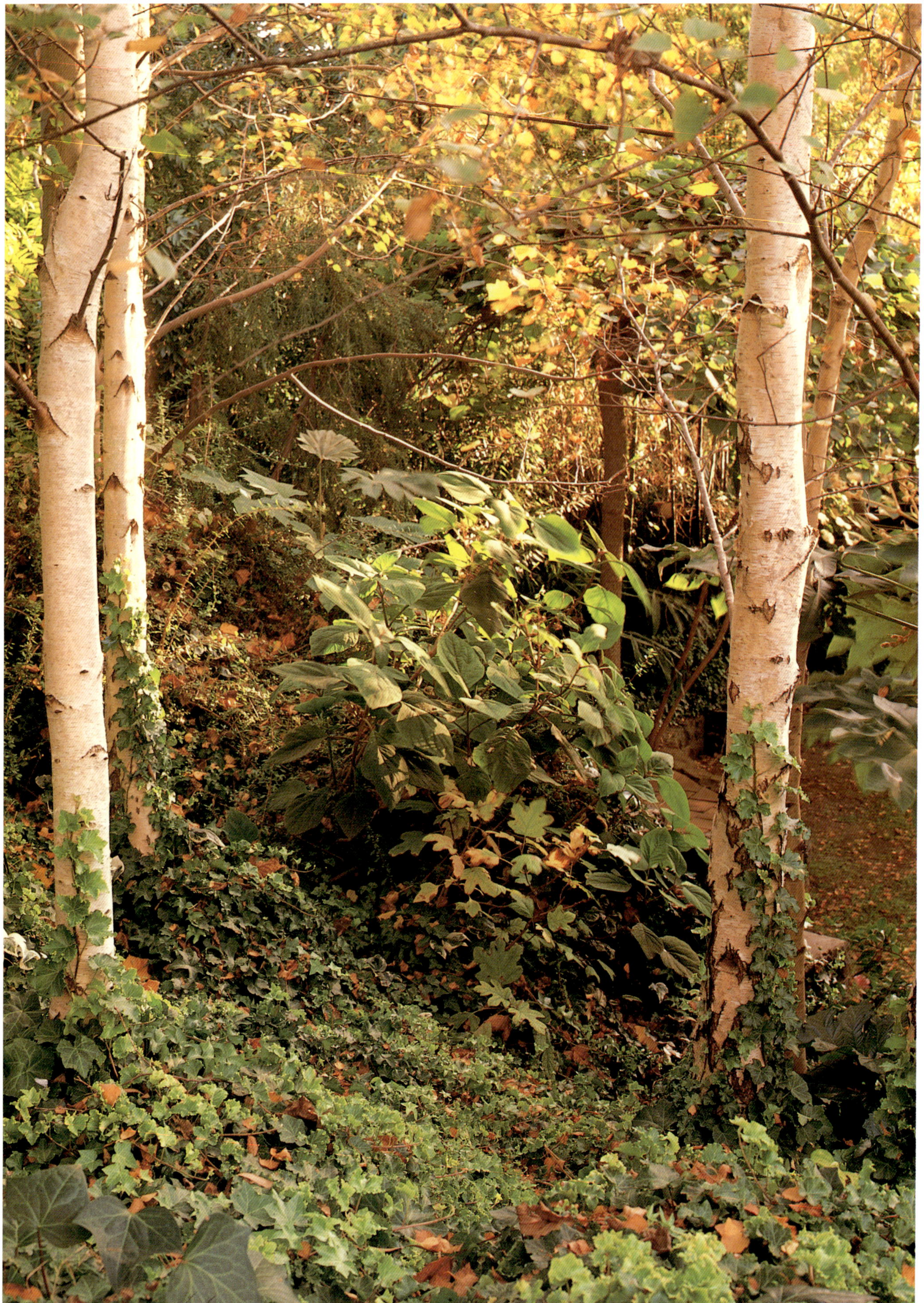

GROUNDCOVERS

The idea of covering the ground with low-growing plants is not really new — lawn is a groundcover and we've had lawns for centuries — but the use of ankle-high plants for the purpose is a relatively recent development in horticulture.

That a carpet of close-growing plants will cut down on the need for weeding is certainly true; but to think of groundcovers simply as a labour-saving device is akin to regarding the living room carpet as merely something to hide the floorboards. Just as a carefully chosen carpet can tie the furnishings of a room together, simple groundcover plantings can bring harmony and aesthetic unity to the various elements of the garden.

Beneath trees, they allow the lines of the trunks and branches to rise uncluttered from the ground; they can flow around and between shrubs; and simple panels of groundcover, in combination with paving and perhaps lawn, can diversify and soften the floor of a patio without actually creating an enclosure.

The key to their use is simplicity; you *can* make intricate patterns of several species, but one or two always looks better. And since you are going to be putting in a lot of them you need to choose carefully.

IF YOU DECIDE to blend several groundcover plants to make a pattern, try to choose ones of similar vigour — otherwise, unless you constantly intervene, the more invasive will crowd out those more sedate in habit.

Choosing plants

A good groundcover should be reasonably permanent; if you have to be lifting or dividing it every year or two you might as well plant annuals (some of which, like verbenas and alyssum can make very pretty short-term groundcovers); it must look attractive, or at least presentable, all year; and it goes without saying that it shouldn't be susceptible to attack by pests and diseases or temperamental about where it will grow. It should be capable of making a sufficiently tight cover to be weed-proof, without being so rampant that it will become a nuisance itself.

In the early stages, you may not save all that much work; groundcovers need the soil prepared as well as any other plant. Especially, their bed *must* be free from perennial weeds like couch, oxalis and onion weed; if they take hold before the groundcovers have closed in, you'll never get them out. Groundcovers may be able to hold their ground against invaders — they can't seize it from them.

SINCE MOST GROUNDCOVERS need close planting — only 35 cm or so — for reasonably quick cover, you'll need a lot of plants. Nurseries often give a discount for quantity, but buy them small or propagate them yourself for economy.

ABOVE: Vinca major variegata, *a first-rate groundcover, asking only to be trimmed in late winter for neatness.*

BELOW *'Meadow gardening', using a mix of perennial flowers, with bulbs and the odd annual thrown in, as groundcovers is set to be the latest gardening craze. It certainly looks pretty here, but it is far from no-work gardening.*

OPPOSITE: *The words* groundcover *and* ivy *are almost synonymous in the minds of many gardeners. It's a good plant — but don't let it run up trees as is happening here.*

LEFT: *The matched avenue along the country garden driveway may be a cliché but it always looks attractive. These are flowering plums — a tunnel of scented blossoms in spring.*

BELOW: *A collection of unusual varieties of trees can be as fascinating to the gardener as one of lesser plants — and every bit as easy to overdo. These are mostly varieties of the Japanese maple, Acer palmatum.*

TREES

Trees are the most important plants. Larger and longer-lived than any other living things, they bestow a sense of permanence to a garden in a way that the more ephemeral shrubs and flowers never can. And more than anything else, they create the mood of the garden, whether shady and secluded or open and sunstruck; some of the most satisfying gardens are composed of just trees and grass.

Yet many people get cold feet about planting them — trees will get too big, they say; they'll cast too much shade, or not enough; they'll find the gutters with leaves and the drains with roots; and they take *forever* to grow.

Think of trees in relation to people, and their placement and selection becomes much less intimidating. Think of smallish, bushy ones to mass for privacy; of shade trees to walk and sit under; of trees just to look at, maybe framing the house or a view; of deciduous trees where you want the sun in winter and shade in summer; and evergreen where you need year-round greenery.

Choose trees for their purpose

When you've decided the roles you want your trees to play in the garden, you can start to think of the best species and varieties for your purposes. Think of flowers, of autumn colour, of the beauty of bark and the lines of

LEFT: *In a very large country garden, massed deciduous trees rising from a floor of* Hypericum *groundcover make a forest as enchanting as any in a fairy tale.*

FAR LEFT: *The slender spires of cypresses frame the tower of a grand house and emphasise the formal, symmetrical character of the garden. Their almost black darkness contrasts with the silver foliage at their feet.*

LEFT: *The Japanese cherries* (Prunus serrulata) *are a froth of scented flowers in spring and colour nicely in autumn. But choose your cultivar carefully — some are most inelegant in growth, like blown-out umbrellas. They like a cool climate.*

BELOW: *The spring flowering* Magnolia liliflora *is not so much a tree as a vastly overgrown shrub. Others, like M. denudata and M. salicifolia are more arborescent in habit, and with careful pruning will develop trunks tall enough to allow you to walk under them.*

branches, of precise tones of green, whether light or dark, of whether the roots are deep enough to allow other plants to grow beneath, or whether this doesn't matter.

Beware of sentiment — just because you have happy memories of the willow in your grandmother's garden doesn't mean that a willow will be the best choice for yours, though of course it might. And don't fall into the common misbelief that evergreen trees never drop any leaves — they do, a few at a time, for much of the year. The tidy-minded might prefer a relatively short period of raking up in autumn.

We are all impatient, and very fast growers are always a temptation, but they have a habit of being either short-lived (like most wattles) or in a hurry to get really big, like poplars and many eucalypts. Treat them with caution. Moderate growers don't really take all that long — plant them as early in the garden-making process as you dare and they will have grown up before you know it.

IT IS POSSIBLE to buy 'advanced' trees from specialist nurseries, as much as 6 or 8 metres tall. The selection is often limited and they aren't cheap, but the instant maturity they lend to a new garden can make them well worth investigating. Planting them is a big job, perhaps best given to a professional.

Remodelling an existing garden

If you buy a house with an established garden, it's often wise to wait a year or so before you make major changes. If you're planning to alter the house, you might want to wait until your plans for that are finalised; but in any case it takes a little time to see how the garden really works, and if it requires more maintenance than you want to give.

SPRING BULBS might suddenly appear; that dowdy shrub in the corner might prove a real beauty when its season comes around; the patio might turn out to be too small or a hotbox in the first heatwave.

Let in the light

In the meantime, you can probably busy yourself with the pruning shears. Trees and shrubs have a habit of becoming overgrown without it being noticed, and thinning the crowns of trees, trimming tall shrubs (often the removal of lower branches can turn them into useful small trees, gaining light and planting space beneath) and removing overgrowth that's shading windows and making the rooms gloomy are usually all overdue. But go easy — after all, wasn't the garden one of the things that attracted you to the place?

What to remove, what to leave

You'll probably find quick-growing plants that have come to the end of their lives and are due for removal. Easy — out they go. But what about the desirable ones that are simply too big for their places? Will you take them out too, or can you plan around them, maybe adjusting the line of a path or extending the patio in another direction to make up the loss of space? Make your decisions slowly; it takes only an hour or two to remove a tree, years to replace it if you change your mind.

ABOVE: *Snapdragons: planting annuals can be a way of satisfying the urge to do something in the garden while you wait and see what it is going to do.*

BELOW: *You might be lucky enough to find a treasure trove of rare bulbs like these double daffodils.*

WHEN THE OWNERS *of this terrace house took over, there was not so much a garden as a disaster area (above left). Low budget dictated slow progress, but a year later, with some paving installed and an odd assortment of plants donated by friends, it is beginning to look like a garden.*

Remodelling an existing garden

ABOVE: *Six months after moving day, the floor of the garden has been laid — paving on two levels, with a bark-chip mulch in the narrow area at the side of the house.* RIGHT: *Three years after, tree ferns and palms have grown to make a tropical oasis.*

LEFT: *A fuchsia presented by a friend.*

ABOVE: *The side area, with an informal path of stepping stones across a freshly-laid mix of gravel and tanbark.*

RIGHT: *Two years later, the bare bones softened by a mix of herbaceous plants — Japanese anemones, montbretias and daisies.*

79

COLOUR IN THE GARDEN

It is possible to decorate a room entirely without colour, using neutral tones of grey, beige, or white, and to do it beautifully too.

But not a garden. Before you introduce a single plant, there is colour there — from paving, from the blue sky overhead, from the near and distant landscape, from the soil itself. Then the house is coloured (if only in neutral tones) and there's the vivid green of grass and the darker one of trees — you couldn't design a garden without colour if you wanted to.

Flourishing like a green bay-tree
Psalm XXXVII

In a sense, the all-green garden is the equivalent of the all-beige room. The green of leaves is so much a part of the natural landscape, and of gardens too, that we often think of it as just a neutral background for the jewel-bright colours of flowers. (How often have you heard it said that a garden 'lacks colour', when what is meant is that there aren't enough flowers?)

Green is a colour too
Green is a colour capable of great beauty and subtlety; even the commonest plant is not a uniform block of tone the way a painted wall or a sofa is — it is filled with highlights and shadows as each leaf catches the light in its own way. There are changes with the seasons as new leaves take on the tones of maturity, and each species has its own particular tone — some brilliant green, some darker, more greyish, more olive.

A beige room can be merely 'safe' and dull — but a luxuriant green garden is unlikely to be. In any case, it won't be *entirely* green — there will still be the colours of pavings and the house (which are unlikely to be green) for relief. And there will be flowers, unless you carefully exclude them — and even if you do, many trees, and most shrubs and groundcovers, produce flowers in their season.

BELOW: *The contrasting textures, shapes, and tones of leaves can be as exciting as flowers, as here at Wollongong Botanic garden.*

RIGHT: *Against the cream walls and honey-coloured woodwork of the house, the varied greens in this garden take on a velvety richness. The little sphinx brings the colour of the walls into the garden which isn't always all green — in their seasons come the shocking pink of azaleas, pots of summer annuals in sunny corners, and the autumn gold of the elm tree (a little too close to the house considering the vigour of its roots?).*

= Colour in the garden =

Use bright colours as highlights
In a basically neutral-toned room, you can add highlights of colour — a cushion here, a lampshade there, a painting over the mantelpiece. In the same way you can use the jewel colours of flowers as highlights on the green background of the garden. Flowers always draw the eye. Place them to emphasise the important points in your design: around the patio; to guide the eye to the front door; to lead it away from eyesores.

A garden's colour scheme can never be static; flowers are not with us for long, but each season brings new ones. Flower colours are easy to play with — you might balk at the idea of flame-red cushions on a purple sofa, but a flame rose like 'Super Star' could look rather well lording it over a clump of purple irises, the green of their leaves diluting the clashing colours. And if you don't like the effect after all, it's a simple matter to shift one or the other plant out of the way at the appropriate transplanting time.

As in decorating and clothes, garden colours go in and out of fashion. At the moment, all-white gardens are popular, and the sunset tones of yellow and orange are frowned on by some would-be taste makers; but ignore fashion. Plant the flowers you like, in the colour combinations you like.

> THE ENGLISH ARTIST John Piper (he did the windows in Coventry Cathedral) was once asked how he planned the colours in his beautiful garden. 'Rigid colour schemes,' he said, 'are as useless in gardens as they are in paintings.'

RED

The opposite to green in the spectrum, red is the most eye-catching and exciting colour of all. It comes in a wide and dramatic range of tones, from the pure fire-red of cannas to the muted crimsons common in roses (which provide the widest selection of any flower), but it is a dark colour and shows up best against a background either lighter (like these cannas against the light grass beyond) or an even darker one. Red flowers often have an orange or a purple undertone; try to keep the two apart or they'll scream at each other.

ABOVE: *Snapdragons come in all tones of red, from copper to crimson as well as pinks and yellows.*

BELOW: *Red on red: the fire of verbenas against duller red bricks. But does the yellow conifer strike a false, shrill note? Maybe a rich, dark green shrub would have been better.*

FAR LEFT: *Though we usually grow them to eat, scarlet runner beans have bright flowers.*

LEFT: *If you want to go in for red in a big way, nothing beats bougainvillea, here swamping a yellow Spanish broom.*

BLUE

Blue, really blue, flowers are rather rare. Most 'blue' flowers veer towards mauve and lilac, and are often somewhat grey in tone. On their own, they can appear to recede into the green background; they need contrasting companions to show them up.

What to choose? Just about anything. Clear pink and purple companions will make them look bluer; salmons and yellows tend to bring out the mauves, but are themselves intensified; and blue flowers with grey foliage can give an effect of cool delicacy. Beware though, of pastel schemes in the strong sunlight of an Australian summer — they can easy look washed out in the glare.

SINCE SOFT BLUE FLOWERS go with almost anything, they are valuable for separating clashing colours where white would be too stark, and for tying a kaleidoscopic, cottage-garden mix together.

ABOVE: *Sometimes disparaged because it is so very easy to grow,* Plumbago auriculata *makes a chest-high, billowing cloud of powder blue flowers.*

RIGHT: *Not permanent or solid enough for the garden framework, the blue daisy (*Felicia amelloides*) is wonderful for filling in with cheerful flowers which it produces most of the year. It grows ankle-high.*

To me the meanest flower that blows can give
Thoughts that lie too deep for tears
Wordsworth

RIGHT: *While the mauve-tinted blues are anything but assertive, pure blues are eye-catching. Here two pools of* Lithospermum *hold the eye before it travels down the path, where a change of direction is heralded by the rich pink of the rose.*

PINK

Pink is the commonest colour in flowers. Like red, it comes in warm tones (coral and salmon) or cool (rose pinks and candy pinks, with their hint of mauve) which can clash; though the paler the tone, the happier the two families of pink will be together. Coral pinks go happily with yellows and oranges, mauve pinks with purples, blues, and cool, pale yellows (mauve pink seems to be the colour nature loves most of all, bestowing it in an infinity of flowers from old-fashioned roses to petunias to pink boronias and spring blossom).

SPRING BLOSSOMS *can have you swimming in pink, if only for a short time. They are all cool, blue-toned pinks; be careful with the strong yellows of daffodils or calendulas which will clash — and the blossoms don't provide any green to calm things down.*

Where you tend a rose a thistle cannot grow

THE CRIMSON *of a climbing rose, with a supporting chorus of cool colours — cream foxgloves and mauve-blue catmint.*

YELLOW

Many gardeners are prejudiced against yellow flowers, and it's true that they can be so brilliant that they shout any neighbour down. But blend several tones of yellow together, maybe extending the range to coral-pink and orange, give your chorus some bass-notes of darker tones (red, dark blue or purple, or the dull bronze of a *few* coloured leaves) and you will have a sight which will make up in cheerfulness what it might lack in subtlety.

Be careful with your backgrounds though — especially if they are artificial; yellow flowers tend to make red bricks look crude, and concrete shabby. Pale yellows in the cream-to-lemon range can lighten a mixture of darker colours, whether it be of warm or cool tones.

> YELLOW MAKES its appearance in leaves as well as flowers. Many variegated plants have yellow patterns on their foliage, and there is an abundance of 'golden'-leaved conifers. They need to be used with circumspection (as do 'red'-leaved plants) if they are not to look gaudy and artificial.

RIGHT: *Grey foliage is valuable for blending colours and gentling bright flowers into the overall pattern. Here lambs' ears (Stachys) calm down a mass of yellow daisies and orange lilies. Most grey plants need plenty of sunshine.*

BELOW RIGHT: *The combination of gold and blue is as striking as any. Here gazanias play the starring role, supported by blue lobelias.*

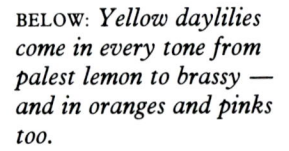

BELOW: *Yellow daylilies come in every tone from palest lemon to brassy — and in oranges and pinks too.*

ON A BROAD BANK *sloping up from the house, a brilliant mix of annuals and perennial daisies in every shade of yellow, cooled by the blue-green of iceplants and creeping junipers.*

Colour in the garden

ORANGE

Mid-way between yellow and red, orange has much of the warmth of yellow, but not quite its degree of brilliance. Orange flowers can often fit where yellow would be too sharp; and of course, it is the dominant colour in autumn foliage.

ABOVE: *Asiatic lilies (this is 'Enchantment') bring the drama of hot colours to the summer garden. Plant them at the feet of spring-flowering shrubs to keep their roots cool.*

TOP LEFT: *Tulips in orange and gold glowing against the soft greens of grass.*

TOP LEFT: *In mild climates, the marmalade bush* (Streptsolen jamesonii) *makes a feast of orange every bit as good as the deciduous azaleas of cool climates. The ranunculi are close in tone — but some bold, clumpy foliage would have introduced a contrast of form and texture.*

BOTTOM LEFT: *Desert flowers are always dazzling in colour, and none more so than the orange mesembryanthemum* (Lampranthus aurantiacus). *Here its brilliance is foiled by the grey tones of the railway sleeper wall.*

85

Landscaping your garden

ABOVE: *See how the designer, having decided on only white flowers to avoid upstaging the magnificent marble urns, has avoided dullness with varying forms and tones of foliage.*

ABOVE RIGHT: *Touches of white, mainly white roses (the white furniture too) will show up in the evening; by day they add crispness to a planting in reds, blues and pinks, all set against the greens of year-round shrubs and trees.*

RIGHT: *A green and white scheme carried out in every detail, with white walls and furniture and almost-white paving (top). The rich purple of violas is the perfect foil to the white and yellow Chrysanthemum paludosum (bottom).*

WHITE

White can be something of a prima donna. In small clumps it can purify and tone down clashing colours; in masses it can be so dazzling that it takes over. White flowers come in all tones; stark and brilliant in camellias against their dark leaves; faintly green in white daffodils; touched with ivory or pink in white roses; spangled with the gold of the centres in many daisies. All look cool and elegant against the garden's background of green, and white-and-green gardens have been a fashion for years.

BECAUSE IT REFLECTS so much light, white shows up after dark, and if you're planning to make much use of the garden in the evenings you'll want to include many white flowers.

White-variegated leaves are liable to burn in hot sun; take the hint and use them, with discretion, to bring light into heavily shaded corners.

Children's gardens

A child's dream — trees to climb, rough grass to run on, secret places to hide — and no fancy plantings to get in the way of Rambo and Fido...

Plan for your children

Children vary in their needs and temperaments as much as adults do — and their desires change with alarming speed as they grow up. Sandpits and jungle gyms are a bit like toys — the centre of a child's world today, but tomorrow — 'what, *me*, play with such childish things?' So think carefully before investing in any of the playground-style equipment that you see in the shops; however well made and designed, it has a limited life. Very young children need a secure place to play while you keep an eye on their safety — a securely fenced yard-within-a-yard. Give it a soft surface, tanbark or a thick (at least 10 cm) mulch of bark chips or old leaves. It doesn't take much of a fall onto hard ground, let alone paving, to cause a serious injury. Plan it with an eye to the future; when it is no longer needed as a playground, can it become a vegetable garden, a herb patch, an extension of the patio or a place for a teenager to pull apart a motorbike?

Wheeled toys — tricycles and scooters — really need a hard surface. Certainly, a child can go round and round on the patio, but the fun soon palls. Could you create a mini-grand prix circuit with paths right around the garden? Would linking the various areas — patio, lawn, vegie garden or what have you — with paths help in the running of the garden in any case? Would such a system of paths help tie the whole design together? Once they grow into bicycles, let alone motorbikes and cars, the children are on the threshold of adulthood and their needs in the garden are those of adults. But then their need, and yours, for a quiet retreat from the world is greater than ever — and where better to indulge it than in a leafy and friendly garden?

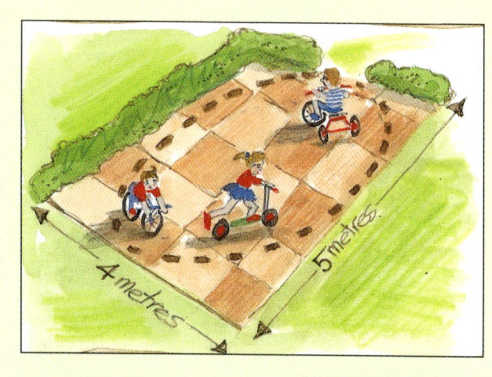

A TRICYCLE *can turn on a 1.2 metre circle or stay on a 60 cm path, but more generous space is desirable. For several trikes and go-carts — or mini-bikes — you need at least a space of 4 by 5 metres just to go round and round without pile-ups.*

A SANDPIT *contained by heavy timber, sanded smooth to avoid splinters. The seat is a nice idea; Mum would find it a comfortable place to read a story. There's shade, and the rest of the child's area is given a soft surface of shredded bark. Poisonous and prickly plants are, of course, kept well away.*

BELOW: *Nasturtiums.*

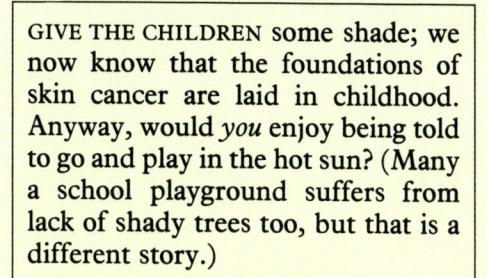

GIVE THE CHILDREN some shade; we now know that the foundations of skin cancer are laid in childhood. Anyway, would *you* enjoy being told to go and play in the hot sun? (Many a school playground suffers from lack of shady trees too, but that is a different story.)

GARDEN CONSTRUCTION

Patios and terraces, pergolas, swimming pools, fences, pathways and steps are all major garden construction jobs. You may want to hire a contractor to do some or all of it (see Getting it on the ground, *page 24) or you may decide to tackle everything yourself. In any case, the decision on what structures you want in your garden should be made early in the planning stages. No use planting some fine trees just where you later want your pool.*

POOLS AND PONDS

Water is more than just an excuse for growing waterlilies. Sparkling in the sunlight or lying still and quiet in the shade it is endlessly beautiful and fascinating.

Whether you choose to create a natural pool or display water in a frankly artificial way, keep its setting simple, so that it can sparkle like a jewel on velvet. It's fatally easy to overdo the waterlilies, quaint rocks and Japanese irises.

Learn from nature

It takes art to make a naturalistic pool look really natural. This is not an art that can be described; you'll learn far more from a few hours in the bush seeing how nature does it than from a torrent of words. But at least make your pool a generous size — a puddle is no ornament to anything. Site it at a low point to which water would naturally flow.

Art is that in which the hand, the head, and the heart of man go together
Ruskin

'A GARDEN WITHOUT WATER,' a Persian poet said, 'is like a beautiful woman with her eyes closed.' A garden composed simply of trees, grass and water can be completely satisfying — low on maintenance too. Why don't we see more such gardens in our hot climate?

THE LARGER YOU *can make a cascade the more convincingly natural it will be; but you need to use substantial rocks — in nature, little ones get washed away. Rockwork as grand as this is not for the do-it-yourselfer. If you have to use cement, keep it well back from the rock faces — otherwise nothing destroys the natural effect faster.*

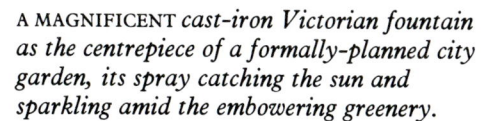

= Garden construction =

TOP LEFT: *A formal pool can be quite tiny, as long as it is in proportion to its surroundings, like this one at the side of a patio. The raised edge not only keeps people from backing chairs into the water, it invites you to sit and admire the goldfish.*

TOP RIGHT: *A polished stone sphere, once the finial of a gatepost, now presiding over a raised pool. The spiky leaves of the water iris are just the right contrast.*

ABOVE LEFT: *You don't have to have ponds and fountains — the water in this basin sitting on a fallen log brings sparkle to a bushland garden — and the birds like it too.*

A MAGNIFICENT *cast-iron Victorian fountain as the centrepiece of a formally-planned city garden, its spray catching the sun and sparkling amid the embowering greenery.*

RIGHT: *Stepping stones can be fun, though they call for a large pond if they aren't to look silly. Use flat stones, at least 35 cm wide, and set them about 30 cm apart. For safety's sake, they must have a firm foundation, and an alternative route to the other side would be wise.*

Landscaping your garden

BOTH PATIOS *use the same area of paving, but B feels more spacious, both because the area is broken up and extended by planting and because it leads you further out into the garden.*

BELOW: *A house with a lot of glass almost cries out for a patio extending the living rooms. Here both patio and house are well shaded by trees, and the patio is decorated with shade-loving pot plants. The arrangement of the paving bricks in circular patterns contrasts nicely with the angular lines of the house.*

PATIOS AND TERRACES

The word 'patio' comes to us from Mexico and California, and originally simply meant a courtyard — the paved central courtyard of a large colonial house or *hacienda* where much of the activity of the household took place. We rarely build our houses around courtyards these days, and the Spanish word has come to mean a paved part of the garden devoted primarily to outdoor living. Sometimes we use the English term 'terrace', either way it suggests a paved level area, handy to the house where we can put out furniture without getting muddy underfoot.

Consider the sun and wind

Of course we want the patio sheltered from the wind and shaded from the hot summer sun — though it would be nice if it caught the winter sunshine — and we want it big enough to be useful, not merely a path-like strip of paving beneath the living room windows.

A patio needs to be more spacious than an indoor living room; it isn't just that we like the idea of 'the great outdoors', we do need more room outside. We walk with longer strides, our gestures are larger, we prefer to sprawl in a deck chair rather than sit primly upright. Six people can dine in reasonable comfort in a room three metres by three and a half, but a patio that size will seem crowded with four people sitting around a table.

AS A RULE OF THUMB, whatever shape your patio may be — you're not confined to rectangles — its smallest dimension shouldn't be less than three metres, allowing for encroachment on the space by foliage.

Where to put it

Ideally it would be the north side of the house as it's easier to control the sun there, but you can make a comfortable patio on the east, west or south sides too. It's more important that it relate comfortably to your living rooms,

== Garden construction ==

maybe to the kitchen too. You will be taking guests there, and it would be nice not to have to lead them out through the bedrooms or the laundry.

If the design of the house allows it, it is always pleasant to be able to step straight out onto the patio through wide doors, so that it becomes physically an extension to the living room (or the family room, or the dining room) breaking down the distinction between indoors and out, as modern architects are so fond of saying. But you may prefer to set your patio further out into the garden, perhaps to catch the sun or to take advantage of a fine view — or maybe just so that you can get away from the house and among the trees and greenery.

The shape of the land may suggest a spot too. There are no 'rules' — the right spot is where you will feel most comfortable.

> AS YOU MAKE your plans for a patio, take out a chair or two and sit for a bit to try your ideas out. You'll soon know if you've chosen a good spot, and what you'll have to add in the way of plantings, shade, or whatever to make it perfect.

BELOW: *Almost detached from the house and shaded by blossoming crabapple trees, this patio forms the focus for entertaining in a large garden. The expanse of brick paving is broken up by panels of groundcovers and a path leads off in the foreground to destinations unknown.*

TOP LEFT: *This patio opens onto the driveway at the side of the house via a substantial gate. As well as being a place for sitting out, it also serves as an entry garden for the owners who use their 'back' door much more than their official front door. The use of timber duckboards over the drain (instead of a cast iron grate) is a pleasing detail.*

BOTTOM LEFT: *In this garden, the veranda and the patio are separated by planting; the indirect route between the two makes the small garden feel bigger. The patio is the entire garden; shaded by deciduous trees, it has a pool with waterlilies as its focal point. The floor is made of blocks of timber with hardwood strips for pattern.*

BARBECUES

Before you plan a permanent barbecue, ask yourself how much use it will get. If you only cook out a few times each summer, you might be better served by a portable model which can stay out of the way in the garage or the shed when its services aren't required, and which can be set up in a different part of the garden each time.

On the other hand, setting up the portable and then putting it away becomes a chore if you have to do it frequently; to have your barbecue ready and waiting can be a great convenience. And you can build extra work space into it, which saves having to cart out a table for the cook's accessories, plates and bowls.

Don't be too ambitious

Essentially, a barbecue is just a fireplace, and it needs, like an indoor fireplace, to be built of masonry which can take the heat and the weather. Here lies the difficulty, for a clumsily designed barbecue can be a monsterpiece, dominating its garden like an altar waiting for sacrificial virgins. The secret is to make it as small as possible (it's amazing how much food even a small portable can turn out — do you really need something capable of feeding fifty people?), and to site it carefully in association with something more eyecatching than it is: maybe a fence with creepers, a wall, even a massive tree.

People love to cluster around the cook, so make sure there is room for them to mill around with their plates and glasses, as well as to sit and eat; and if you can arrange for shade so much the better. (Slaving over a hot stove isn't fun in the hot sun, and any patio is best shaded at lunchtime.) Grass will wear out under barbecue traffic, so paving is called for; and if you can use the same material, or a harmonising one, for the barbecue itself, it will help bring all into aesthetic harmony. You may want to make the work top out of polished stone or tiles for easy cleaning.

HERE IN AN INFORMAL *garden, the barbecue has been given a terrace of its own, large enough for the cook and his helpers, and separated from the main patio where people sit and eat by steps and a light screen of tree ferns.*

A WOOD-FIRED BARBECUE *can end up as a fairly massive structure, what with the need to provide somewhere to store the wood and the desirability of a chimney. This one, built against the brick boundary wall (notice how it is in dark bricks, which don't show smoke and grease marks), is the focal point of quite a small garden.*

SWIMMING POOLS

Swimming pools may no longer be only for the very rich, but they still aren't cheap — if you decide to have one, be prepared for it to be much the biggest item in your landscape budget.

The size

It's easy to be tempted into extravagance by the glossy brochures put out by the swimming pool companies, and you need to be very clear-headed about what your needs are. Will you want to swim laps for the exercise, which is just about the best there is; or will you (and the kids) be content just to splash around? Lap swimming calls for a minimum clear length of 12 metres (40 feet) — more is better — but for horsing around you only need about half that. Either way, the width is pretty much a matter of appearance, though less than about 3 metres (10 feet) will be rather cramped.

The shape

Modern methods of construction will allow any shape, but beware of making a fussy outline in the hope that the pool will look like a natural waterhole — a simple, regular form is not only more economical to build, it almost always fits in best with the rest of the garden. If it helps gentle the pool into the landscape, you can bring grass or plantings almost up to the edge — allow a metre or so of paving between planting and the water unless you fancy the idea of a swim whenever you need to go gardening — but you really ought to have a generous 'beach' of paving around at least half the perimeter. Link the beach to your main patio and you're well on the way to creating a pool which looks as though it belongs and wasn't an afterthought. Make sure, though, the poolside area drains *away* from the pool, or the filter will have to cope with dirty water every time it rains.

Pool fencing

Until very recently, you could put your pool anywhere you pleased as long as the yard itself was securely fenced; but now regulations in many places call for a separate enclosure with a childproof fence and gate. Ask your local council for advice — you are going to need their approval before you can build in any case. The need for enclosure does limit your scope; but with ingenuity you should be able to find ways to minimise the impact of the fence — suitable plantings perhaps — or you could make a virtue of necessity and make it a feature of your design.

The site

Of course, you'll want the pool in as sunny a spot as possible, and shelter from the wind will add many days at either end of the swimming season. It's nice to have shade nearby to retreat to, even if it's only a beach umbrella set in a socket in the pavement. Normally, the pool goes in the backyard for privacy, but if your contractor can't get in there with his equipment — an important consideration — or if the front garden seems a better location, by all means think of putting it out front. You'll need to look carefully at the privacy aspect; the council may not take kindly to the idea of high walls or fences.

A SIMPLE ROUND POOL *makes a serene foreground to a bushland view. The timber decking is just right where bricks or concrete would be too hard and formal.*

ANOTHER SIMPLE POOL, *set at a lower level than the umbrella-shaded terrace. If you bring planting right up to the edge like this, be sure it won't be in too much danger of being splashed, especially if it is a salt-water pool; even chlorinated water isn't good for plants.*

Spas and Hot Tubs

A spa or hot tub isn't just a miniature swimming pool, its pleasures are of a different kind: more relaxed, quieter, more intimate even; bathing rather than swimming. Perhaps that's why most people find a much greater degree of privacy, even seclusion, desirable than for a pool.

AS THE WATER is heated anyway there's no need to site a spa in the sun — it could be under a pergola or enclosed completely in a pavilion — but shelter from cold wind is essential.

Because it's small, it's relatively easy to create the illusion of a natural pool with surrounding rocks and the sort of jungly plants that will enjoy the steam and humidity; but don't forget to allow a paved (or timber-decked) area next to the spa large enough for people to sit and talk to the bathers. As with pools, spas should be fenced off for safety.

A hot tub is just an oversized barrel made of timber; you can sit it on paving and climb into it, or build a deck around it. A spa is made of fibreglass or concrete and is sunk into the ground. They can be custom-designed, but it's much cheaper to buy one off the peg and design around that. Make sure you can get at the various pumps and filters for maintenance, but this usually poses little trouble, the manufacturer will advise you. Check with the local council; your installation may require their approval.

PLACED AT ONE END *of a deck outside the living rooms, and with the pergola extended out over it (see plan below), this lattice-enclosed spa is simultaneously part of the house and the garden. Notice how, by allowing the spa to stand above the deck, a seat could be built in all around.*

THERE'S NO REASON *why you can't build a spa ensuite with a swimming pool and have the pleasure of a cold plunge to follow. Here the elaborate tiling of the spa contrasts with the much plainer treatment of the pool.*

IN A COLD CLIMATE, *a small courtyard, roofed in clear fibreglass or acrylic, can become a 'conservatory' allowing the spa to be enjoyed all year. This one is in Canberra, and is a little unusual in being placed at the front of the house. The warmth allows subtropical plants to be grown, in this case palms, orchids and tree ferns, though the ferns' habit of shedding clouds of dusty spores into the water causes frustration at times.*

Floors and Paving

In interior design, a successful room starts with the best floor you can afford. This is much less true in the garden; out of doors our line of vision is higher than when we are inside; we are more aware of trees and shrubs and the sky itself than of the floor of the garden room. This is not to say that the choice of floor doesn't matter; a garden will feel different according to whether its floor is of grass, fallen leaves, gravel, or paving. (Bare earth, dusty in dry weather, muddy in wet isn't really an option, as nature will demonstrate by trying to cover it with weeds.)

LEFT: *Bricks, laid in herringbone pattern, their edge masked by allowing groundcovers to trail over it. This is the strongest bond for brick paving and is used in the Netherlands for paving streets.*

BELOW: *Basketweave is probably the easiest pattern if you are laying bricks yourself — it allows you a certain amount of inaccuracy before it looks careless. And it's decorative.*

SECTIONS *of log, set in a bark mulch.*

LEFT: *Slate always looks glamorous — it should, it isn't cheap — but you need a textured finish or it can get very slippery when wet. Here it is combined with grey bricks.*

ABOVE: *Gravel, much used in Italian gardens, makes a pleasingly neutral background to plants, and if you choose a river gravel it looks more expensive than it is. Here it is stabilised with lime (roll in about 10 per cent of hydrated lime and water it in) to make a driveway.*

RIGHT: *Three different flooring materials combine in harmony in this garden — lawn, the timber deck which raises the outdoor sitting room to the floor level of the house, and a mulch of rocks beneath the trees. These aren't very comfortable underfoot; you could substitute gravel to extend the patio, or lay a carpet of lush groundcovers.*

*Consult the Genius of the
Place in all
That tells the water whether
to rise and fall*
Alexander Pope

GRASS GROWING *between the paving blocks can give a marvellously soft and romantic look, but your paving units need to be large enough that they don't disappear altogether as the grass tries to creep over them. This path — it could well be expanded into a full-size patio — is made of wide slabs of hardwood.*

Flooring materials

The choice of floor is as much a matter of the use you will make of it as of visual considerations. Grass (not necessarily maintained as velvet lawn) is cheap, comfortable to walk or play on, and a flattering background to both plants and people, but it stays wet after rain, and wears out under concentrated traffic. Gravel looks pleasant and earthy, but isn't good to walk on in bare feet; it must be laid on a fairly level surface or it washes away. Fallen leaves, which you might augment with bark chips, are appropriate in a woodsy sort of garden, but tend to track into the house. Hard pavings — stone, brick, concrete — will take any amount of wear and traffic, don't mind being put in the shade as grass does, and are the choice for patios and well-travelled paths. But they aren't cheap, and your budget will have a big say in which you choose. Don't let that inhibit your design; plan your paved areas generously, even if you have to make do with brick rather than stone, concrete slabs rather than brick. A generous, comfortable patio will look luxurious; a skimpy one, no matter how expensive the paving material, will always feel mean and cheap.

IT CAN BE TEMPTING to make patterns of different materials as though you were designing a carpet, but remember that a plan tends to give the pattern of the floor an importance that it may not have in reality, and a few years of dirt and weathering will tone it down considerably. As plantings mature they will be the most eye-catching feature of the garden in any case.

96

STEPS AND WALLS

Unless your land really is billiard table flat, the chances are that you'll be dealing with a change of level somewhere. Turn it to advantage, making it mark the division between two garden rooms or activities — between the patio and the lawn, the front garden and the street, a cultivated and a 'wild' area.

Retaining wall

Probably there will be a bank of soil between the two roughly level areas; you can hold it with planting (groundcovers come in to their own here) or by building a retaining wall, welcoming its strong horizontal line, which can be softened with plants if you wish.

Retaining walls, whatever their material (brick, stone, concrete, rough timber) need to be substantial and to look it; professional advice (from a landscape architect or a builder) is worth seeking, especially if the wall is going to be more than about half a metre high.

TOP LEFT: *A pleasingly informal use of heavy timber for both steps and retaining walls, in harmony with the unpretentious architecture of the house. Vertical timbers like these needs to be buried for at least a third of their length for stability. The soft-coloured paving bricks tone with the grey of the timber; red bricks would have been too assertive.*

CENTRE LEFT: *Outdoor steps need to be lower and easier than inside, and the relationship of riser to tread is all important. The rule is that* twice *the riser plus the tread (in centimetres) adds up to 66. The ideal is a 12 cm rise and 42 cm tread, but you can vary according to the formula. Try to keep your risers less than about 16 cm, with 18 cm as the absolute maximum, when a handrail would be a good idea.*

FAR LEFT (top): *The lines of any construction can be softened by plants. Here the Mexican daisy (*Erigeron mucronatus*) cascades over the top of a stone retaining wall.*

BOTTOM LEFT: *Though you can build a retaining wall vertically, sloping it back (battering) gives greater strength. You need to ensure that water can drain from behind, either by allowing weep holes at the base, or putting rubble and a drain there, or its pressure can endanger the stability of the wall.*

FAR LEFT (bottom): *A change of level between lawn and patio becomes the centrepiece of the garden.*

Landscaping your garden

Steps

Steps have to do more than just look pretty — their purpose is to get you from one level to the other in comfort and safety. Whether you aim for a formal, architectural look or a casual and rustic one, you need to pay close attention to their proportions. Their width is a matter of appearance (as long as you aren't cramped; don't forget to allow for encroaching plants); a short flight usually looks best if its width is as generous as possible, while a long one needs to be narrower if it is not to be too imposing. But the relationship of riser to tread is critical, and one of the few places in garden design where you need to be to-the-centimetre accurate in calculations and measurements. If your steps don't fit the human gait comfortably, sooner or later someone will come to grief on them.

It goes without saying that they must be securely built; a wobbly stone, or an edge out of level or uneven, is an invitation to disaster, and so are steps that get slippery when they're wet. (Be careful with tiles, polished slate, even bricks in damp shade where algae grow.)

ABOVE: *The retaining wall at right is so completely clad in* Trachelospermum *that its ugly concrete blocks are quite invisible. The path is just stepping stones through the groundcover.*

RIGHT: *Billowing masses of Mexican daisies soften the lines of a rather imposing flight of stone steps. They would obscure them entirely if they weren't trimmed back each winter. The daisy (*Erigeron mucronatus*) was a great favourite in colonial gardens.*

LEFT: *Here is another way to use timber, either thick baulks of hardwood or old railway sleepers. Running the steps parallel to the wall makes them less dominating.*

RIGHT: *A detail of a patio, paved in brick, with railway sleeper steps and rocks to hold the slight change in level.*

PERGOLAS

We mostly see a pergola as a kind of vine-roofed veranda attached to a house, and very attractive it can look too, its lines often adding distinction to what would otherwise be a very ordinary facade. But the usefulness of the pergola to the architect shouldn't make us forget that it really belongs to the garden.

There's no reason why it can't be detached from the house and placed where you need shade and can't wait for a tree to grow. (Vines grow faster, and shadecloth can stand in for the first couple of years.)

Make your pergola sturdy
Either way, the first requirement is that the structure must be *strong*, both to the eye and in reality; a wisteria in full growth is awfully heavy when it's wet with rain. If you make it in timber, let the posts be at least 15 cm square — 18 cm is better — and the beams in proportion. What with the sun, the rain, and wet vines, pergola timbers are very much exposed to weathering, much more so than any timber in the house. Even with the most durable wood (hardwood or treated pine), you should make a regular check along the tops of the beams and renew the paint or preservative before rot can start.

The spacing of the beams is a matter of proportion; but if in doubt, space them wider rather than closer — you can always train the young vine shoots on strings. Whether you shape the beam ends or cut them square is up to you. Be guided by the style of the house; garden structures always look better if they harmonise with it. The same goes for the finish — the usual rule is to paint or stain to match the woodwork of the house. Though timber is traditional, there's no need to confine your designs to it. Free-standing pergolas especially, can look handsome with pillars of brick or stone, even with classical columns (in concrete these days); and steel can lend itself to airy arched shapes. If you're planning anything other than a simple structure, though, you will find the advice of a landscape architect or an architect invaluable.

Other structures
Structures for vines aren't the only ones you might consider; you might think of gazebos or summerhouses of greater or lesser elaboration, arches over a gate or path, or the old-fashioned garden shed. (Old-fashioned because most of us seem to keep our garden tools in the garage nowadays.)

GARAGES AND CARPORTS properly belong to the house rather than the garden, and if you need to build one you're best to consult an architect (or at least a good builder) rather than try to design it yourself.

ARCHING OVER A PATH *with creepers makes a shady tunnel of greenery — maybe flowers too. The roof needn't be continuous; here just a few arches create the effect.*

THIS SUMMERHOUSE *started out as a redundant clothes hoist. Now, covered with Burmese honeysuckle* (Lonicera hildebrandiana) *it is a shady retreat for adults and a playhouse for children. Heavy timbers prop up the corners or the whole thing would collapse under the weight of the vines.*

NOT A PERGOLA *in the usual sense, this graceful steel and canvas structure makes an elegant transition between the house and the garden designed to echo its severe modern lines. Plants would spoil it.*

*G*ardens and secrets seem to go together

LEFT: *An entrance arch in the modern idiom, signalling the entrance in a fenceless front garden.*

RIGHT: *Here timber slats are used to cast the shade; they could work in tandem with vines on the open section of the pergola. The pale stain on the timber keeps the effect light and airy; dark brown might be oppressive.*

LEFT: *Steel tubes from the curves of this pergola belonging to an ultra-modern house. It's covered with ornamental grapes, still young, and perhaps when they grow the abrupt juxtaposition with the timber pergola won't be quite so obvious.*

Garden construction

FENCES AND ENCLOSURES

A fence to a cattleyard is there to keep the cows *in*; a garden fence is intended to keep uninvited people (and their animals) *out*.

But if you have a new house and a bare backyard, the fence, rarely tall enough to give you real privacy, is apt to create the feeling that you are just being penned in; and you sense that there are other pens beyond.

The first temptation is to make the fence itself more pleasant to look at, either by substituting a more attractive design, or by adorning it with climbing plants. There are situations where this is appropriate, but others where it is like pinning a figleaf on a statue, drawing attention to what you want to conceal.

Look again; the 'walls' of the garden room are really the trees next door, the sides of the neighbours' houses and the hills in the distance — the fence is only one of the things that create a sense of enclosure. Plant trees to screen the houses and shrubs, and climbers to mask the more obtrusive parts of the fence, and you take away the cooped-in feeling. The eye can enjoy the pleasant views beyond, and the garden feels more spacious.

Putting fences in their place

A timber paling fence is easy enough to hide, but the corrugated iron traditional in some parts of the country isn't; the metal reflects too much light. A coat of paint in a camouflage colour is a great help. It's useful for the flanks of garages and sheds too — but choose dark brown, khaki, or dark grey rather than any shade of green, which is liable to kill the tones of foliage near it. (The lurid shade of 'landscape green' favoured by the makers of chain wire can stand out far more than the plain wire.)

RIGHT: *The fence is only part of the 'walls' of your garden room (top). You can soften it with vines (centre) or plant trees (bottom).*

ABOVE: *Lattice makes an ideal dividing screen, solid enough to frame space, open enough not to completely hide what lies beyond. The arched opening is an unusual detail, but not hard to build.*

ABOVE: *A slight change of level between the front lawn and the street is held by a railway sleeper wall, with the rustic post-and-rail fence above it; flowers and scented plants spill beneath the fence on both sides. Brushing against a scented plant like rosemary or a peppermint geranium would be rather a pleasant incident on the walk to the shop.*

POST-AND-RAIL *fences like this are always associated with the country — and what could be more charming than this one with annuals spilling out through it onto the footpath? You might use low shrubs, even roses if you are sure their thorns won't pose a danger to passers-by.*

Front fences

The front fence is seen from the street as well as inside, and has a public duty to at least not be ugly. Whether it should give privacy depends on your needs — and on the local by-laws; many councils insist on something low if not transparent. If you're tempted by high fences or walls, remember they aren't called 'the burglar's friend' for nothing.

Perhaps it's because we are all so used to the idea that a fence marks the property boundary, that we rarely build them *inside* our gardens. Yet a fence can serve as a useful garden room divider, taking up much less space than a row of tall shrubs. Security not usually being a worry (except with swimming pool fences) you can allow your imagination free play, making the fence as plain or fancy, as solid or as light and transparent as you like. Just don't make it so flimsy that it blows down in the first strong wind.

LEFT: *The seat that you pick up and move around like a wheelbarrow to catch the sun is an old idea. Handsome examples like this one suggest it's due for a revival.*

RIGHT: *Tucked away among the foliage, a terracotta birdbath makes a pleasing abstract sculpture. The grevillea nearby is prickly enough that the cat will think twice about lurking under it.*

ORNAMENTS AND FURNITURE

Ever since people have been making gardens, they have been putting pieces of sculpture and furniture into them, and for the very good reason that both are an invitation to enjoy the garden. A sculpture invites you to come over and have a closer look, a seat to sit for a while. A sculpture doesn't have to be a full-length statue; it might be a Victorian marble bust, a Chinese vase, an old chimney pot — anything that takes your fancy and that will be able to stand up to the weather. But it needs to be fairly large if it isn't to be swallowed up among the foliage. Place it where you want to draw the eye: at the end of a path, beyond a group of trees, in a corner where finding it will be a surprise. But give it a simple setting where a riot of vegetable colours and textures won't upstage it; and if it's at all valuable, fix it in place securely lest it be stolen.

Furniture

Outdoor living calls for somewhere to sit, and maybe for a table on the patio. It's easy to clutter up a garden with too much furniture; you might like to have a small setting ready for the family, augmenting it with chairs brought from inside, even with cushions on steps. A retaining wall or the edge of a raised bed makes a pleasant seat too if it's about 45 cm high and a generous width.

A BEAUTIFULLY *understated bench. Its immaculate joinery goes well with the formal slate paving. The use of the same gravel between the slabs as for the floor in the adjacent area is a nice touch.*

RIGHT: *In a Japanese garden, the traditional water bowl for visitors to wash their hands. This one, carved in the likeness of a Chinese coin, is old and valuable. The austere setting of stones and just a little foliage sets off its beauty.*

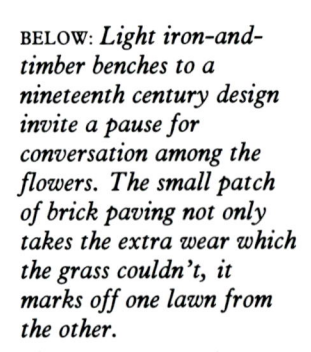

BELOW: *Light iron-and-timber benches to a nineteenth century design invite a pause for conversation among the flowers. The small patch of brick paving not only takes the extra wear which the grass couldn't, it marks off one lawn from the other.*

LEFT: *At the edge of a patio, a pair of terracotta jars display lines as strong as any modern sculpture.*

BELOW: *The finer the sculpture, the plainer its background can be. Trees, a bit of trellis, some gravel — the simplest of settings, made memorable by the magnificent marble statue. It's an idea that could be adapted to the smallest and plainest of gardens, though most of us will have to be content with a reproduction sculpture.*

LIGHTING THE GARDEN

At any time of the year, evening is delightful in the garden; the heat of the day has gone, perhaps there's a breeze, and as shadows deepen even the most prosaic garden takes on a touch of romance. It would be a pity to deny yourself its enjoyment simply because it's too dark to find your way around.

No need to try to turn night into day; it's sufficient to concentrate the light on the areas you'll use the most and leave the rest of the garden to the moon and stars. Of course, you'll want to light up the path to your front door, remembering that your visitors are not as familiar with the way as you are; and steps anywhere in the garden should be lit for safety's sake. But beyond that, it's a matter of the mood you want to create. You might light up a group of soft-leaved shrubs, pinpoint some favourite flowers or pot plants, or maybe backlight a clump of bold foliage to make dramatic shadows. (Beware of training a spotlight on dense dark greenery — it makes no picture at all.)

Lighting for a party
If your patio is outside the living room, you might well find the light spilling through the windows is sufficient; for a party you could augment it with a lamp brought from indoors (waterproof extension cable, please, and not if there's the slightest chance of rain) or even with candlelight or hurricane lamps.

Safety
Remember that electricity and water are a potentially lethal combination, and any electrical installation must, by law, be carried out by a licensed electrician. There are do-it-yourself, low voltage lighting kits available, and they do have the advantage that you can experiment with the positions of the lights until you get them just right; but even with these, professional installation is wise. Peace of mind is well worth the cost.

WATERING SYSTEMS

A built-in watering system is something of a luxury — you can water a garden perfectly well with a garden tap and a hose. Better, with several strategically placed taps and hoses; short hoses are less cumbersome to handle than long ones, they last longer, and you can set more than one sprinkler at a time.

But there's no denying that a built-in system is very convenient. Even the cheapest do-it-yourself kits come with an accessory programmer that allows you to set and forget, and the degree of sophistication available (as the price goes up) is extraordinary: you can choose when any given sprinkler will come on, how long it will run, arrange so that the water goes just where you want it, and all for weeks or months in advance. You can even get programmers that sense whether the soil is dry and water when it is.

Choosing sprinklers
The sprinklers themselves come in three main types:
Tricklers (drippers), the most economical with water, just dribbling it out at the roots of the plants (you need a lot of them, and they're most useful in permanent plantings where they won't be in the way as you cultivate).
Mini-sprays (sometimes called micro-jets) which are like small sprinklers, usually spaced about a metre apart; like tricklers they use very fine pipes and have an irritating tendency to clog up (a filter is essential unless you're very confident of the cleanness of your water supply). They usually stand about 35 cm above the soil and can look as though a convention of sorcerers have been sticking their magic wands around the place.
Sprinklers, which range from small ones covering about a metre and a half to monsters capable of watering a football field. The best are the *pop-ups*, which jump up when they are turned on and then retire discreetly to ground level when the job is done. They are the only kind to use on a lawn.

THERE ARE TWO WAYS *of treating light fittings in the garden — either conceal them completely under foliage, behind stones or what have you, or choose a handsome lamp and display it like a piece of sculpture against a simple background. Lighting designers have come up with few modern designs for garden lights as attractive as this Victorian lantern.*

THE LANTERN IS HELD *high enough to catch the gloss on the leaves of the* Garrya *behind it; if it were lower, the effect would be gloomy. In full bloom, the long tassel-flowers of the* Garrya elliptica *shimmer under artificial light. It's a shrub for cool climates, where it is practically indestructible.*

ABOVE: *Geraniums, easily propagated from cuttings.*

BELOW: *This summerhouse was built in the early 1920s of recycled materials — free then, but costing money now. Still they are cheaper than new, and you might look out for used bricks, stone and timber at demolition yards.*

Costs and budget

How much does it cost to make a garden? Alas, that's a far from simple question. It depends on so many things — how big it is, how elaborate and grandiose (what price upstaging the neighbours?), whether you buy your plants in full bloom, as big as possible, or beg cuttings from your grandmother. Materials and labour (as well as land) vary enormously in price around the country, and in these days of economic uncertainty costs change so fast it's hard to keep up with them.

But it is possible to give a rule of thumb. An average-sized suburban garden, made to a reasonable standard, costs about as much as a car. But what sort of car? That depends. If you live a Mercedes-Benz lifestyle, you probably won't have much difficulty imagining a Mercedes-priced garden; if a Volkswagen is more your budget, then you can make a VW-priced one. Doing all the work yourself, rather than hiring the labour, does save you money (about 60 per cent, very roughly) — and that probably brings you to a good used car price. But it's still in that sort of area.

Estimating costs

Do as the professional designer does; work it out from your plan, measuring it off. So many square metres of paving, so many covered by a pergola, so much grass, so many trees, so many shrubs, and so on. Don't forget so many cubic metres of soil to shift around. Here you see one of the benefits of taking the trouble to make a plan.

The hard part is getting the figures to play with. How much does a square metre of brick paving cost? How much is a shrub? Go and have a look at materials at building information and home improvement centres; they can often give you a price range. Look at the price tags on plants in nurseries. Ring up the manufacturers who advertise in magazines like 'Better Homes and Gardens', the gardening magazines (of which there are many) and 'Landscape Australia': they're usually happy to tell you how much their products cost, and can often give you an idea of how much the installed cost might be. (These sums have a nasty habit of adding up to more than you had hoped; make yourself a cup of tea and take a few quiet minutes to recover.)

Is the cost worthwhile?

Does a nice garden add value to the property? Yes it does, but how much depends a bit on what sort of garden it is. Buyers don't like the idea of buying costs and work, so a low-maintenance garden will always be a better selling point than a labour-intensive one, and so will a well-designed, generously livable one.

Legal matters

In making your garden, you aren't hedged about by laws and regulations to anything like the same extent as you are when you build, but there are a few things to bear in mind.

First, your garden must be confined to your property. If your trees encroach on your neighbour's land, he has the right to remove the intruding branches to a point immediately over the boundary; whether he has to return them to you or has to dispose of them himself varies from state to state — your local council can advise you. (You have the same right with regard to his trees of course; but it's neighbourly to talk it over before you do anything — it doesn't make for harmonious relations if the first time he meets you you're up in his favourite tree brandishing a saw.) And if the roots of your tree damage his house or paving, or clog up his drains, you could be liable for the cost of repairs; likewise if water runs off your property onto his — be careful about the drainage if you are planning major earth-shaping. (Remember too that in most places it's illegal to drain your storm water — this includes your house gutters and downpipes — into the sewer lines.)

The footpath in front of your land is public property; if you want to do any gardening there, you'll be wise to seek your local council's approval first.

> BE CAREFUL with any planting that might obstruct the public, *especially* thorny things like roses or bougainvilleas on front fences; you will be held responsible if a passerby is injured.

Similarly if you want to beautify the common property of a flat or townhouse; talk to the Body Corporate first.

Second, any structures you might build — fences, pergolas, sheds, swimming pools — will need the approval of the local council. Have a talk to their planning department at the design stage; they should be happy to explain any requirements they might have, and whether there might be preservation orders on any of your existing trees.

Third, you can't interfere with the services to your house. It's unlikely that you'll find manhole covers for the sewer or the water on your land, but there may well be overhead electricity or telephone wires, as well as water and gas meters and lines. Talk to the relevant authority if your plans might affect these.

Fourth, you're not allowed to plant illegal plants. These vary from state to state, and as well as the noxious weeds you wouldn't dream of planting anyway, might include such plants as pampas grass, water hyacinths, the dangerously poisonous rhus tree — even bananas, which are forbidden to home gardeners in much of Queensland (they harbour diseases with might infect the commercial crop).

Check with your state department of agriculture, who will also be able to advise you if you will be obliged to spray fruit trees against pests like fruit fly. And if you buy plants interstate, make sure you're allowed to take them home — both Victoria and South Australia have regulations on the matter.

Fifth, remember that you are responsible for the safety of your guests, including people like encyclopedia salesmen and the gas company's meter reader. Public liability insurance can be a comfort, but it won't prevent accidents on slippery paths or unlit steps.

ABOVE: *A composition in pure colours — white, gold and blue. All the plants are daisies. Ephemeral perhaps, but how many of life's great joys are as fleeting as flowers?*

ABOVE: *Why pine in a warm winter climate for the tulips you see in European garden books when sparaxis will out-dazzle them? Part of happiness in gardening is being content with what you* can *have.*

LEFT: *Grand vistas and bold effects may please; but so do intimate close-ups like these primroses. The stepping stone path invites you to linger and enjoy the flowers at your feet.*

Index

Page references in **bold type** indicate the chief reference to a topic, and include both text and illustrations. Page references in *italic type* indicate illustrations.

A

Acacia 59
Accidents 107
Adelaide *46*, 61
Advanced trees 26, 77
Aleppo pines *31*
Aloes *34*
Alyssum *63*
Anemones *22*, *79*
Annuals **73**
  flower gardens 46
  planning *19*
  streetside 40, *41*
  while remodelling *78*
Appleberry 72
Aquilegia *14*
Arches *99*, *99*, *100*
Arctotis *56*, *63*
Arid climate *see* Dry climate
Asiatic lilies *85*
Aspect 28–9
Australian gardens **42–3**
Australian Institute of Landscape Architects 14
Avenue 76
Axonometric projection 16
Azaleas *30*, *65*, *71*, 73

B

Backyards, long and narrow 53, *53*
'Bald' housefront *40*
Bamboo 56
Banks *98*
Banksias 59, *60*, 62
Barbecues *92*, *92*
Bark chips 87
Basket-weave paving 51, *95*
Bauhinias 37, *70*
Benches *103*, *104*
Bent (grass) *30*
Billardiera 72
Birches *38*, 51, *51*
Birdbaths *13*, *46*, *64*, *103*
Birdhouses *13*
Birds 13
Bird's eye view 16, *22*
Blue **82**, *82*
Blue daisy *82*
Bluebells *58*
Body Corporate 107
Boronias *83*

Bottlebrushes *39*, 59
Bougainvillea 56, *81*
Boundaries 37
Box *30*, 71, *72*
Bricks
  lawn edging *31*
  paths *33*
  patios *98*
  paving *26*, *45*, *51*, *53*, *90*, *95*
  terraces *45*
Bridges *33*
Brisbane 33, *39*
Broom *81*
Budgeting 106
Bulbs *54*
Burmese honeysuckle *99*
Bush gardens *see* Native plants and gardens
Bushfires 49
Bushland gardens **47–50**
  seaside 63
By-laws 12

C

Cactus *20*
Californian poppies *31*, *41*, *55*
Callistemons 59
Camellias *30*, 71, *71*
Cannas *81*
Carpentry costs 26
Carports 99
Cars *37*, *38*, *52*, *52*, 99
Casuarinas 62
Catmint *68*
Cherries 77
Children 7, **87**
Chysanthemum *86*
City gardens **51-3**
Climate **28-33**
Climbing plants *39*, 72, *72*
Climbing roses 52
Coleus 51
Collector's gardens 61
Colonial gardens *43*
Colour **80-6**
  edible plants 65
  fences *101*
  pergola *99*, *100*
Common property 107
Conservatory *94*
Construction **88-105**
Contractors 14, **24-7**
Coreopsis *55*, *68*
Corner site *9*
Corrugated iron fence *101*
Costing 106
  landscape contractors 15
Cotoneasters 13

Cottage gardens
  blue flowers 82
  colonial gardens 42
  green *21*
  modern gardens 43, *66*
  structure *73*
Council regulations 12
  encroaching trees 107
  front fence 37
  pools 93
  spas 94
  streetsides 40, 107
Courtyard *48*
Crabapples 13
Creek, artificial *33*, *33*
Creepers *39*, 72, *72*
Crepe myrtles 37, *70*
Cypresses 77

D

Daffodils *54*, *78*
Daisies
  colour *82*, *84*, *107*
  lawns 55
  paths *14*, *41*
  remodelling garden *79*
  walls and banks *97*, *98*
Daylilies *39*, *73*, *84*
Deciduous trees 77
  light and shade 29, 30
  native gardens 60
Delonix *28*, *33*
Desert flowers *85*
Design-by-post services 15
Designers **14-15**
Designing **6-15**
  checklist 19
  plans **16-23**
  planting 68
  water saving 34
Dianthus *35*
Dichondra *52*
Diosma 71
Dividing space *10*
Doodles *18*, *18*, 23
Doors
  front 36
  into garden 91
Drainage 12
Drippers *105*
Driveways
  as boundaries 37
  costs 26
  flower gardens 46
  patios *91*
  planning *38*
Drought-resistant plants 35, *35*
Dry climate 31-2, *31-2*, *34*

108

Index

E
Earthworks 10, 26
Easy-care gardens *see* Low-maintenance gardens
Electricity
 safety 105
 wires 107
Elm trees *51, 53, 80*
Estimating costs 106
Eucalyptus 77
 birds 13
 dry climate *31*
 front gardens *38*
 native gardens 59
 subtropical garden *33*
Evening, flowers for 86
Evergreen trees 29, *37*
Everlastings *35*

F
Family 7
Federation houses
 fences *67*
 hedges *72*
Fees for landscape contractors 15
Fences **101-2**
 children's gardens 87
 climbers *72*
 dividing spaces 10
 Federation cottage *67*
 post-and-rail *102*
 swimming pools *93*
 teatree *72*
 terrace house *39*
Fescue 30
Fires 32, 49
Flamboyant tree *33*
Floors 95-6
Flower gardens **46**
 colonial *42*
 colour highlights *81*
 designing *18*
 gravel paths *32*
Flowering plums *37, 60, 76*
Footpaths 40, *40*
 regulations 107
Formal gardens **44-5**
Fountains *89*
Frangipani *22*
Freesias *54*
Front door *36*
Front fences 120
Front gardens **36-41**, 46
Fruit trees *45*
Fuchsias *19, 79*
Furniture **103-4**
 colour *86*
 long narrow backyards *53*

G
Garages 46, 99
Garden rooms 8, 44, *44*
Garden sheds 99
Garrya *105*
Gates *51*
Gazanias *37, 55, 56, 62, 84*
Gazebos 99
Geraniums *41, 58*, 73, *106*
Gold *84, 85*
Golden elm *53*
Golden rain tree *38*
Grapes *72*
Graph paper *17*
Grass *see* Lawns
Gravel *42, 79, 96, 96*
Great War 42
Green 80, *80*
Grevilleas
 birds 13, *13*
 hedges 71, *71*
 native gardens 59, *60*
Grey foliage *84*
Groundcovers **74-5**
 city gardens *52*
 design 7
 drought-resistant *35*
 low-maintenance gardens *58*
 trees *77*
Gymea lily 13, *62*

H
Hakeas 13
Hammock 7
Handrail *97*
Hebes 30
Hedges **71**, *72*
Heights of plants *68*
Herbaceous border *42*
Herbs 7, *64*, 65
Hibiscus 70
Highlights *81*
Hillside gardens 32, **47-8**
 see also Sloping sites
Hippeastrums *26*
Historical societies *67*
Hobbies 7
Hollow trees 13
Honeysuckle 99
Hoses 105
Hot tubs 94
House
 colour *80*
 designing the garden 9
Hypericum 77

I
Illegal plants 107
Impatiens *21, 37,* 51
Indian laburnum *33*
Indoors, bringing outdoors
 dining 6
 glass rooms *90*
 living room *26*
 location *91*
 long narrow backyard *53*
 movement between house and garden 10
Informal gardens **46**
Insects 13
Insurance 107
Irises *15*, 81
Iron lace *39*
Ivy 51, *74*

J
Japanese anemones *22, 79*
Japanese cherries 77
Japanese gardens 30
Japanese maple *76*
Jasmine *72*

K
Kangaroo paws *60*
Kerbside verges 40
Kitchen gardens **64-5**
Knox, Alistair *60*
Koelreutias *38*
Kolwitzias *70*
Kurume azaleas 30, *73*

L
Laburnum *33*
Lambs' ears *84*
Landscape architects, contractors, gardeners 14
Landscape Contractors' Association 14
Lanterns *105*
Larkspurs *41*
Lattice *101*
Lavender *68*
Lawns **96**
 adjoining patio *97*
 become popular 43
 brick edging *31*
 eliminating 56
 groundcovers 75
 low-maintenance *54-5*, 56
 mowing *54*, 56
 temperate climate 30
 water 34
 when to plant 27

Index

Laws 12, 107
Leaves 96
Level areas 10
Light
  see also Shade
  remodelling gardens 78
  vegetable gardens 64
Lighting 105, *105*
Lilies *84*, *85*
Lime (fertiliser) 12
Lithospermum *82*
Lorikeets *13*
Low-maintenance gardens *8*, **54–8**
  front gardens 39
  hillside gardens 47
Low planting 10

M

Madagascar periwinkles 37
Magnolia 77
Mallawok (estate) *42*
Mantanoas *14*
Maples *76*
Marguerites *35*, *73*
Marmalade bush *85*
Masonry costs 26
Meadow gardening *55*, *75*
Melaleuca *70*
Mesembryanthemum *85*
Mexican daisies *97*, *98*
Mini-sprays 105
Montbretias *79*
Mowing *54*, *56*
Multi-level gardens 47

N

Narrow backyards *53*, *53*
Nasturtiums *87*
Native plants and gardens **43**
  birds *13*
  dry climate *32*
  low-maintenance gardens 59–60, *59–60*
  water *35*
Nature strips 40
Neighbours *9*, 107
Noxious weeds 107
Nurseries 14
Nurserymen 14

O

Orange (colour) *85*, *85*
Ornaments **103–4**
  flower gardens *46*
  kitchen gardens *64*
  planning *24*

ponds *89*
Outdoor rooms *see* Indoors, bringing outdoors

P

Painting fences *39*, 101
Paling fences 101
Palms *33*, *79*
Pandanus tree *33*
Parking *38*, *52*
Parrots *13*
Parsley *65*
Pastel colour schemes 82
Paths
  brick *33*
  flower colours *82*
  formal gardens *44*
  front gardens 36, *38*
  grass *45*
  gravel *42*
  hillside gardens *48*
  informal gardens *46*
  public 40, *40*, 107
  replacement 12
  stepping stones *79*, *107*
Patios **90–1**
  adjoining lawn *97*
  brick *98*
  bushland gardens *49*
  entrance 36
  low-maintenance gardens *58*
  subtropical climate gardens *33*
  temperate climate gardens *30*
Pavilions *48*
Paving **95–6**
  brick *26*, *45*, *51*, *53*, *90*, *95*
  colour *80*, *86*
  costs 26
  drives *38*
  grass between *96*
  groundcovers *75*
  replacement 12
  stone *37*
  swimming pools *93*
Pear trees *60*
Pelargoniums *12*
Pergolas *14*, *26*, *94*, *99*, *100*
Period gardens **66–7**
Periwinkles 37
Perspective drawings 16
Petunias *18*, *22*, *83*
Photographs *67*
Pines *31*
Pink *46*, *83*, *83*
Piper, John *81*
Pittosporum *60*
Planning **6–12**
  checklist 19

children's gardens *87*
front gardens 36–29
hedges *71*
hillside gardens *48*
low-maintenance gardens *56*
patio *91*
plant height *68*
planting *68*
trees *76–7*
Plans **16–23**
  garden rooms *45*
  scale 16
  spas *94*
Planting **68–77**
Plumbago *82*
Poinciana *28*
Ponds **88–9**
  city gardens *52*
  kitchen gardens *65*
  patio *91*
Pools *see* Ponds; Swimming pools
Poplars 77
Poppies *31*, *41*, *47*, *55*
Post-and-rail fences *102*
Pot plants
  city gardens *52*
  patio *90*
  streetside *40*
Prices, quotes for 24
Primroses *107*
Primulas *65*
Privacy
  front gardens 36–9
  hillside gardens *48*
  planning 9, *9*
  pools *93*
  trees *46*
Privet *70*
Proteas *13*, *48*
Pruning 77
Prunus 77

Q

Quotes 24

R

Railway sleepers
  steps *35*, *63*, *98*
  wall *101*
Rainforest trees *42*, *49*
Rainwater 34
Red *46*, *81*, *81*
Regulations 12, 107
Remodelling 78–9, *78–9*
Removing unwanted plants 78
Retaining walls *97*, *97*, *98*
  costs 26
Rocks
  bushland gardens *50*

Index

designing *11*
waterfalls *88*
Roots of trees 107
Rosemary 71
Roses
  climbing 52, 72
  collector's garden 61, *61*
  colonial gardens *42*, *66*, *67*
  colour 81, 83, *83*
  with shrubs 73
Royal poinciana *28*

S

Safety
  electricity 105
  guests' 107
Sandpits 87
Scale of plants 70
Scarlet runner beans *81*
Scent 69
Scheduling 25, 26-7
Sculpture *24*, 103, *104*
Seaside gardens **62-3**
Seats *103*
Security *102*
Selection of plants 68
Shade *28-9*, *29*
  children's gardens 87
  patios and terraces 90
  subtropical gardens 33
Shrubs
  drought-resistant 35
  hedges *10*, 71
  large 70, *70*
  planning *19*
  small 73, *73*
Silver beet *65*
Silver birches 51, *51*
Site 8-9
Site plan *17*, *20*
Slate *95*
Sloping sites 9, 10-11, *12*
  see also Hillside gardens
Snapdragons *78*, *81*
Soil
  groundcovers 75
  planning 12
  seaside gardens 63
  topsoil 26
Solandra *39*
South Australia 31-2, *46*
Spanish broom *81*
Sparaxis *54*, *107*
Spas 94, *94*
Spraying fruit trees 107
Spread of shrubs 70
Sprinklers
  against bushfires 49

watering systems 105
Steep sites see Hillside gardens;
  Sloping sites
Stepping stones
  flower gardens *107*
  paths 79
  ponds 89
  waterfalls 88
Steps **97-8**
  bushland gardens 50
  dividing areas 73
  height 97
  railway sleepers *63*, *98*
Stone paving *37*
Storm water 107
Streetsides **40**
  privacy 37
  regulations 107
Subtropical climate **33**
Summer *28*
Summerhouses 99, *99*, *106*
Sunflowers *13*
Sunlight see Light
Sweet alice *35*
Swimming pools 7, 27, **93**

T

Tanbark *79*, 87
Tanks, rainwater 34
Teatrees
  birds 13
  fences *72*
  seaside gardens 62, *62*, *63*
Telephone wires 107
Television, influence of 43
Temperate climate **30**
Terrace house gardens 25-7, *39*, 78-9
Terraces *45*, 90-1
Terracing 47
Textures *34*
Theme 21
Timetables 26-7
Topiary 71
Topsoil 26
Townhouses *36*, *39*, 51
Toys 87
Trachelospermum *98*
Tree ferns *79*
Trees **76-7**
  advanced 26, 77
  birds 13
  bushland gardens 49, *50*
  choosing 35
  city gardens 51
  easy-care 7
  encroaching 107
  existing 12
  front gardens *37*

groundcovers 75
planning *11*, *19*
privacy *39*, *46*
shade *28*, *29*
simplicity 17
space dividers *10*
townhouses *51*
view *32*, *37*
Tricklers 105
Tulips 51, *85*
Two-level gardens *48*
Types of gardens **44-65**

U

Umbrella *6*
Urns *46*

V

Vanda *10*, *14*
Vegetable gardens *64*, 65
Verandas *29*, *67*, *91*
Verbenas *81*
Victoria 30, *42*
Victorian gardens 42, *43*, 57
Views 66
Vinca 75
Vines 52
Violas *86*
Virginia creeper 52, *72*

W

Walls **97**
  climbers *9*, 72, *72*
Water 88-9
Water bowl *104*
Water saving **34-5**
Waterfalls 88
Watering systems 105
Wattles 77
Weeding 56
Weeds
  groundcovers 75
  noxious 107
White 86, *86*
Wind *29*
  patios and terraces 90
  seaside gardens 62
Window boxes *40*
Winter *28*
Wisteria 21, *39*, 72
Wollongong Botanic garden *80*
Worker's compensation 24
World War I 42
World War II 43

Y

Yellow 84, *84*

Published by Murdoch Books®, a division of
Murdoch Magazines Pty Ltd,
213 Miller Street, North Sydney, NSW 2060

Design: Elaine Rushbrooke
Finished art: Jayne Hunter
Illustrations: James Gordon
Additional photography: Stirling Macoboy, Geoffrey Burnie,
Tony Fragar, Rodney Beames, Roger Mann, Ralph Neale of
"Landscape Australia"

Publisher: Anne Wilson
Publishing manager: Mark Newman
Production manager: Catie Ziller
Managing editor: Susan Tomnay
Marketing manager: Mark Smith
National sales manager: Keith Watson
Picture librarian: Dianne Bedford

National Library of Australia
Cataloguing-in-Publication Data
Mann, Roger, 1948-
Landscaping your garden
Includes index
ISBN 0 86411 203 3
1. Landscape gardening. I. Title.
(Series: Better homes and gardens homemaker library)
712.6

First published 1992. Reprinted 1994.
Printed by Mandarin Offset, Hong Kong
Typeset by Post Typesetters, Brisbane
Text Roger Mann, 1992
© Photographs and illustrations Murdoch Books® 1992

All rights reserved. No part of this publication may be
reproduced, stored in any retrieval system or transmitted in
any form or by any means, electronic, mechanical,
photocopying, recording or otherwise without the prior
written permission of the publisher.

Murdoch Books is a trade mark of Murdoch Magazines Pty Ltd.
Better Homes and Gardens® (Trade Mark) Regd. T.M. of Meredith Corporation

Australian distribution to supermarkets and newsagents by
Gordon & Gotch Ltd,
68 Kingsgrove Road, Belmore NSW 2192